A MANIACAL GAME!

As the first prisoners started forward, weak and staggering from lack of food and water, the officer in charge shouted, "Run! Run!"

We had to run up the passageway, across the boat deck, and down the narrow gangplank. From where I was standing, I couldn't see when someone fell. But I didn't have to. The dreaded report of a rifle signaled the fact that one of our number was dead.

I started to count the shots, but could not continue.

Each bullet is a life snuffed out, I told myself in agony. I can't keep record, as though I'm keeping score in some game!

Run for the West

Bernard Palmer

RUN FOR THE WEST
© 1979 David C. Cook Publishing Co.
All rights reserved. Except for brief excerpts for review purposes, no part of
this book may be reproduced without written permission from the
publisher.

Published by David C. Cook Publishing Co.
850 Grove Ave., Elgin, IL 60120
Cover design by Kurt Dietsch
Cover illustration by Dennis Bellile
Printed in the United States of America
Scripture quotations, unless otherwise noted, are paraphrases or
translations of a Hungarian version put into English.
ISBN 0-89191-132-4
LC   78-72934

CONTENTS

PUBLISHER'S NOTE

The authors of this book remain deeply scarred by the ordeals through which they have lived. Although they want to share their story as a testimony of God's grace and protection, they have insisted on using pseudonyms so as not to endanger the lives of friends and relatives who still live in Hungary and elsewhere.

Bernard Palmer, the professional writer who created this manuscript based on extensive interviews with the family, has given us his full assurance that—except for the changing of names—this is a true story in every respect. We present it to the reading public as a reliable documentary.

PROLOGUE

My name is Sandor Berger. My homeland is Hungary, my heritage Jewish. Since before I went to school my parents had planned on my being a rabbi, but that was not to be. As a young man in my teens, I came to realize that Jesus was my longed-for Messiah. I married a Christian girl and settled down for a quiet life with my family.

But that was not to be, either.

First came the Nazis, and we saw our country ground under the iron heel of Hitler's elite. Neither my Christian faith nor my Gentile wife could prevent my being taken to work camps and eventually to a death camp where American liberators finally rescued me.

I had no sooner regained my health and reestablished my household than the pressure started all over again—this time from the Stalinists. Life was better after the treacherous dictator's death, but a great fear had taken hold of us. The history of Hungary has been bathed in blood for as long as man has been keeping records. Great, plundering hordes from every direction have swept across our fertile land, leaving devastation and death in their wake.

We looked to the past—to what had happened to our fathers and to us—and were sure it would happen again. If not to us, then to our children or our children's children. Even before the war some of us had dreamed of leaving Hungary, but the way had been closed. When the student uprising of 1956 spread from Budapest to most of Hungary, opening the borders for a time, we fled the country, as so many thousands of others had done.

Now I am an old man. I live in the United States with my family. We serve our Lord by sharing God's love with our own people here and abroad in many different but small ways. We have often talked about all that the Lord has brought us through. We have thanked God for his protection, his comfort, and the ability he gave us to hold onto life while people were dying all around us. We do not know why we lived while others did not.

We do know that as we lived through the horrors of those years, we discovered more of what it means to be followers of Jesus Christ. We learned not only how he wanted us to live, but also how he would have us feel and the choices he would have us make in times of pressure and fear and uncertainty. Several times along the way we discovered that we did not know him as well as we thought we did, and many times we were saddened to see just how far short of his desires we came.

My wife, Ester, saw a different side of the war than I as she tried to protect our home. Our daughter, Ida, was twelve when Hitler's legions flooded into Hungary. She and Tibor Vago, the young man who was to become her husband, felt yet different pressures and threats.

Here is our story.

ONE   The Yellow Star

SANDOR

When the Nazis came goose-stepping into Hungary with their pogroms in 1944, those who were considered Jews by religion had to register and wear the yellow Star of David. The rest were to be left alone. In those days many Jews became Christians, at least outwardly, to escape persecution. I had put my trust in Jesus Christ when I was sixteen years old and was married to a Gentile, so I was permitted to continue preaching and working as a tailor.

I didn't talk with Ester and Ida about it, but in my heart I believed that one day the Jews would all be taken from their homes, whether or not they were followers of Christ. I was not surprised when the Nazis began to assign Christian Jews, whom they did not consider loyal enough to serve in the army, to work camps to support the war effort. Early in 1944 I served in one temporarily, but when the work was finished, I was sent home with the warning that I could be called back at any time.

Ida, with the exuberant optimism of children, was sure I would be able to stay at home for the rest of the war. We tried to prepare her for my being taken again, but she seemed determined not to believe it. By this time both Ester and I knew that the dreaded knock on the door would come again. Soon there was another announcement about the Star of David. Every Jew from a family where both parents were Jews by birth was to wear the yellow star, even if married to a Christian. Ester gasped as I reached impulsively for the radio, as though turning it off would somehow cancel the startling words. I smiled sheepishly and pulled my hand back, concern in my eyes. I have never considered myself a brave man and was more disturbed by this announcement than I wanted my little family to know.

"You will have to find a piece of yellow material for me," I said. "I will have to have the star before I can go to the shop in the morning."

Holding back the tears, Ester found some material and set to work. She was not one given to crying. Yet agony was written on her face. She knew as well as I that this was the first step toward open persecution.

She was just finishing the star when further news came from the radio. "Everyone who is a Jew must wear the yellow Star of David unless he is a Christian missionary or minister, or became a Christian before he married a Christian woman. Of course the children must have been brought up by the parents as Christians. Those who meet such requirements do not have to wear the yellow star."

We stared at each other in disbelief. It seemed as though God had instituted that qualification just for me. In all of Budapest there were only a few Christian Jews who qualified for the exemption. Yet there was no question about me. I preached somewhere almost every Sunday, and had been doing so for a long while. The next morning I was one of the few Jews who did not have to wear the yellow star. How we thanked God for that!

It was not long until we began to realize how important that announcement was to us. Those who were wearing the yellow star were being snatched from their homes, the places where they worked, and the streets, to be herded into concentration camps.

However I was only called in for the work force. This time I was taken from the village where we lived, in the suburbs, to a Christian mission school in the city. We were forced to live in the school building and work at the same job as before, dismantling machine tools in local factories so they could be shipped to Germany.

ESTER

I am Ester Schmidt Berger. My parents were Hungarian-born Germans, and papa was a deacon in

the church they attended. They lived in Hungary for
many years. Papa and mama had been born there, but
during World War II they escaped to Germany. Sandor
was already in the work camp, so before papa and
mama left they insisted that Ida and I move into their
home, a block or two from our own.

My husband, Sandor, was never one to ask for
anything. Before the trouble, he was always quiet. I had
to push him to learn what he wanted or needed. It was
the same after the Germans took him the second time.
Every night Ida and I would go to see him at the mission
school and always I would ask what he needed.

"Nothing," he would tell me. "I am fine."

I could see by the clothes he was wearing, the way they
hung on his slight, emaciated frame, the gaunt look in
his face, that he was far from being as well as he wanted
us to believe.

One evening the situation changed.

"Ester," he said, "I don't like to ask you, I know you
have so much to do, but I have a need."

"What is it?" I asked, pleased that I could help him in
some small way.

"My clothes are so dirty, I am ashamed to wear them. I
could do them myself, but I have so many I wash for, it is
hard to get my own laundry done."

I gathered them up quickly. I knew how hard he
worked after hours washing clothes for those confined
to the school who were wealthy enough to pay him. He
did it so Ida and I could have the things we needed. "I'll
bring them back tomorrow night," I assured him.

"And, Ester, I would like a loaf of bread, if you have the
flour and can manage to bake it after you have finished

the washing," Sandor said.

"I will bring two loaves!"

"*Nem!*" He smiled wearily. "One will be enough!"

The next morning I washed his clothes and baked a loaf of bread especially for him. It was a big loaf of rich, dark bread, the kind he liked best. That night Ida and I went back to the school.

However, everything was empty when we got there. The building was dark and quiet. Even the guards were gone. I had been expecting something like that to happen, but not so soon, not without warning. "O God in heaven!" I cried out in agony. "They have taken him away, and he does not even have his warm clothes."

A stranger was coming along the street, his coat collar turned up against the cold and his steps hurried as he made his way toward his home. Seeing Ida and me, he moved to the edge of the sidewalk, contempt glittering in his eyes. Though he did not speak, I knew he was thinking, "What are you, an Aryan, doing here where they have kept Jews? They're gone and good riddance!"

Another passed the building from the opposite direction, and I saw the same scorn in his face. "Why should you care that they're gone?" his eyes demanded as clearly as if he had shouted at me. "They're only Jews!"

I had never known such hot, blinding hatred from strangers. I wanted to attack both of them with my hands. I wanted to scratch their belligerent, ugly faces until they were raw and bleeding, to kick and hit at them until my strength was spent.

Gentle, warm-hearted Sandor was one of those contemptuous Jews! Sandor, who had never hurt anyone, who was kind and loving even to those who held him captive. I knew he would scold me if he were aware of the hatred and rage that flared so suddenly within me.

I do not remember that hatred proudly. It was a cancer in my heart, a poison spreading through my being. I felt dirty and unclean because of it, and yet could not force it away. Not for a long time.

We were still standing in front of the large, empty building when the superintendent of the Christian mission came out. It mattered not to him that I was German and Sandor Jewish. He saw us as two people in love who were separated from each other, perhaps for the rest of our lives.

"They are gone," he told me. "They left this morning. I don't know where they were taken."

I thanked him and, reaching for Ida's hand, started back toward our home in the suburbs.

"Where is papa?" she asked timidly.

I wanted to tell her that he was close by and would be coming back at any moment. But I could not protect her from it. "I don't know," I said simply.

"Is he all right?" she asked fearfully. "Will he come back soon?"

"They have probably taken him to work in some other part of the country for a while," I said, hoping my words were true.

Once we got home, I could no longer hold the tears back, even though I fought them because Ida cried easily and I did not want to upset her. I felt I would never see Sandor again. He would catch cold without his warm clothes, and I knew how ruthlessly they would treat him if he were sick.

Never in my life had I felt so alone, so miserable. I wanted to pray, but my agony was so great I could not. I was sure no one cared; even God had forsaken us.

Weeks later I got a tattered card from Sandor. I do not know how he managed to mail it or how it came to reach me. Our mail service was more uncertain than usual in those days. My heart sang as I saw the familiar handwriting.

My Dearest Ester and Ida,
  I do not know where they are taking us or what is going to happen, but I have been doing much thinking about both of you. It would be easier if you would divorce me, Ester. If you do that and move to Germany with your papa and mama, you will be safe. I can come and find you when the war is over.

Tears burned my eyes. There were many women who were doing as Sandor had suggested so they would escape the persecution that might come upon them.

But I was not going to divorce him. It mattered not whether Ida and I had it easy or difficult. He was my husband and I would carry his name until my death.

TWO Rabbi

SANDOR

The Jews of our country did not have much religion in the days when I was a boy, but my parents were different. My papa went every morning and evening to the synagogue to pray. Some of those who came had to be paid to be there so the rabbi would have the required ten persons present to get out the Torah. But not my papa and mama. They walked with the God of Moses.

There were six children in our family already, before I was born. Mama was in poor health from bearing me, so my papa and mama made a vow: they promised God that if he would heal her, I, Sandor, their youngest son, would become a rabbi. They knew that it would cost much to educate me, but it did not matter to papa. What good was money if the mother of his children was not well?

God answered their prayers, and before many weeks mama was strong once more. True to his promise, papa began to make plans to carry out their part of the arrangement. I had to be properly educated, so when I reached the age of five I was put in a Jewish school to learn Hebrew and the books of Moses. Classes were difficult, but papa and mama saw to it that I learned my lessons.

Overall I enjoyed the atmosphere of Hebrew school. Our learning, however, was somewhat different than the truth—or so I found when I became a believer in Christ and began to read the Bible myself. We were taught only the nice things about Abraham and David and the others in the Bible, things that would make us proud of our heritage.

We were told that Abraham followed God and had such strong faith that God promised to make his descendants as many as the sands of the seashore, but we learned nothing about how Abraham had Sarah pretend to be his sister.

We were read the story of how God gave David victory over the wicked Goliath, but were not told that he also committed adultery and murder.

And we heard about the Messiah. Over and over again we learned the prophecies of Isaiah until we had locked the words in our hearts. The Savior was coming to destroy his enemies and save us. He would establish his kingdom on earth, and we would receive our rightful

places as God's chosen people. How proud we would be
of our Jewish origin!

I learned all those things and more, but papa and
mama soon discovered that of all their children, I was
the least suited to be a rabbi. It was the fault of the
church near the house where we lived. Every Sunday
they sang so loud that by the time I was ten years old I
had memorized most of the songs they sang.

"What a Friend We Have in Jesus" was the one I liked
better than the others. I sang it around the house all the
time, even though papa said he did not like it. It was not
that I tried to sing those songs to go against him. I
wanted to be a son who obeyed his parents. A good boy,
we were taught at our house, brought honor to himself
and his papa and mama. My problem was that the tune
of that song, or one of the others, danced in my head
until I could contain it no longer and it would pop out,
unannounced and unbidden.

Apparently since I was young and papa figured I
didn't realize what I was singing, he never scolded me
hard for it, but he was disturbed. "How can we send that
Sandor to train as a rabbi?" he would ask my mother in
exasperation. "Think how he would shame us by
singing such songs in a place where everyone could
hear—even the teachers. At home it does not matter so
much, but at the school for rabbis—*Ach!*" He threw up
his hands in despair.

Of course I did not know what the song meant when it
spoke about Jesus being a friend. I didn't even think
about the words I was singing. We were taught that
Jesus was against Judaism. I learned differently only
when I was older: that Jesus loved me and wanted to

save me and be my friend. All I really knew in those days
was that I loved the songs I heard coming from the
church and that my only friends were the boys who
went to Sunday school.

I wanted to go to church with them, at least long
enough to find out what went on there and why so many
smiles went in and out of the old frame building, but
papa and mama would not allow it.

"The church is all right for *them*," mama would say,
sweeping her hand in the direction of our neighbors'
homes in a broad, all-inclusive gesture. "But you are
Jewish, Sandor. For you, as it is for papa and me, it is
the synagogue.

"It is enough that your singing of church songs
makes us too ashamed to send you to the school for
rabbis. We cannot also let you go to church so our
Jewish friends point the finger at us."

I did not quite understand everything she was saying,
but something in her manner made me see that I
should go no further. Still, I am thankful for those
church boys. I could not have gone to school without
them.

You must to understand what it was like in those
days. I was a Jew and not everyone liked Jews. Papa
tried to pretend that our Hebrew roots made no
difference to our neighbors. "In some places it matters,
maybe," he would grudgingly say, "such as Berlin or
Vienna or Paris, but not here." He always spoke proudly
about our neighbors. "They are my friends."

Sometimes if a man had too much wine, he would
curse the Jews to papa's face as crooked, lying cheats
who had all the money. Usually, however, it was the

silent treatment: an uplifted eyebrow, a knowing smirk, a remark with a hidden meaning. If it was particularly difficult on a given day, papa might mention what had happened as we sat around the table in the secrecy of our home. Mostly, he held the words in his mouth; only the hurt in his eyes revealed how badly he felt.

But the boys at school were not as careful as their papas. They made fun of us openly because we were not like them and had strange customs they could not understand. We did not eat pork or meat with blood. We had separate dishes for certain kinds of food. In our Hebrew school we learned a language they were unfamiliar with, and we went to the synagague on Friday nights and Saturdays instead of the more acceptable Sunday morning.

Many bigger boys picked fights with those of us who were Jewish unless we brought them candies. That was all right for those whose papas were in the grocery business, but mine owned a saloon. And he did not believe in giving money to his sons. "You can work for it the way I do," he would say. "Then it does not spend so easily."

So the older boys fought with me. It made no difference that I was smaller than the girls of my grade. Almost every night when school was over, two or three of the bigger boys would run after me.

I did not like such fighting, but I had to defend myself, so I kept stones in my pocket to throw when the boys started after me. Once I hit a boy with a rock, and blood oozed out of his head. They came and took me to the judge; but when he found out what was happening, the judge said the law did not allow people to pick on someone just because he was different. The other boys were told that they would be in trouble if they fought with me any more. After that it was much better.

Many of the boys still made fun of me, but not my Christian friends. They treated me the same as they treated each other.

I was not the only one in our family who liked the Christians. Mama and papa were friendly toward them, too. They did not talk to us with the curled lip or the mocking face, and papa liked them because they were honest with him.

"When I buy corn from a believer, I get what I pay for," he said. "They do not say to themselves that I am only a Jew, so it is all right to sell me sticks and rocks mixed in with the grain. What I buy from them is good and of honest measure."

When I was twelve, I had my Bar Mitzvah, which is the custom of the Jewish people. According to our old beliefs, when I finished my training and had gone through the special ceremony, I was to be treated as a man, able to take part in the rituals and observances of our people.

Papa was pleased that I had completed the course of instruction to be confirmed in our religion, and I went through the ceremony dutifully. Neither of us knew that one day I would forsake the religion of our fathers to place my trust for eternal life in the hands of Jesus Christ. Such a thing just did not happen to Jewish boys who were raised in the traditions of their fathers, as I had been raised. Still, papa saw something in me that stopped him from educating me as a teacher of the

Jewish religion. God must have intervened so I would be more free to receive Christ as my Savior.

When the First World War broke out, two of my brothers were taken into the army and sent to the front. One, a printer, was wounded so badly he was discharged and was with us for a few days before going into Budapest to get a job.

"I will take you with me, Sandor," he said. "You can also learn to be printer, no?" Although he was talking to me, he was looking beyond me at papa. But papa, who was never one to make up his mind quickly, would have to think about that.

"It is good," he said after a time. "To learn to print books is an honorable trade."

At the age of fourteen, I cared little whether I was a printer or a sweeper of streets. But if printing was a suitable occupation for my brother, it ought to be all right for me. I had just returned from an unpleasant apprenticeship in another town, but this would be different, I thought. I would have my older brother to keep me company.

I didn't know how wrong I was. My brother took me with him to Budapest, but there his responsibility to me ended. I could stay with him until I got work and had money enough to rent a room of my own, he said, but he did not have time to help me. Printers were scarce during the war and he found a job the first day. I was left to locate work on my own.

Wandering the streets I saw a sign in a window: BOY FROM A GOOD HOUSE IS NEEDED TO LEARN THE PRINTING TRADE. I hurried inside, excited by my good fortune. "I am a boy," I informed the man at the desk, "and we have *two* good houses." One we lived in; the other was the saloon. That, I reasoned, ought to make me twice as acceptable.

"Sit down," the man told me, "and let's talk for a few minutes." Gently he explained that the sign did not refer to the sort of building we lived in. What they were interested in was the sort of family I was from. Had I been brought up to be truthful? Did I lose my temper easily? Did I know how to work? There were other questions—many of them. I don't remember what they were or how I answered, but he must have heard some of the things he wanted, because he hired me.

"If you want to," he said when the interview was over, "you can stay here right away, and start work any time."

I was so anxious to get the job, I scarcely wanted to take the time to go back to my brother's place to get my clothes. I was afraid the man might change his mind.

The printing shop was in a huge building. The main floor was given over to printing, the second housed a church, and the third had a number of apartments and rooms for church members who could not afford a better place to stay. I was given a small space in the room where they stored the paper. It was not very large, and about all I had was space for a bed and a little corner to keep my clothes in. But I was so excited about my new job that nothing else mattered.

At that time I didn't even know the name of the place or what they printed. I soon learned that I had apprenticed myself to a church publishing house, and that their main emphasis was printing Bibles. To me, however, it was simply a place to work, and I threw myself into the new working world.

I was used to being around Christians. And when I did discover what we printed, I didn't even think about it. Later I realized that God had directed me to that place. I had an appointment with him in his own good time, and the printing shop was to play an important role in helping me keep it.

I can't say that I was persecuted while I was on that job, but I noticed little things that set me apart. I had one very good friend who worked there. On the job and in the building after hours, he was always nice to me. However, he would never go anywhere with me, and if we should meet on the street he would walk past me without speaking.

I was shown how to set type, one letter at a time, which was the way it was done in those days, and I was put to work typesetting the New Testament.

I had seen many copies of the Old Testament, and had studied much of it in the Hebrew school, in addition to regular school. Until now, I had never read the New Testament.

And read it I did. I had to read it if I was to be a good printer. After I set a page I went over the proof sheet with care, to be sure there were no errors. I read it over and over again, letter by letter, word by word, line by line. The task of setting type was slow and painstaking, leaving me plenty of time to read and to think about the meaning.

It bothered me to read about prophecy being fulfilled. In Hebrew school and in preparation for my Bar Mitzvah we had studied those same prophecies. Now I was reading them again; only this time they were being fulfilled. I thought much about them, but without any answers that satisfied me.

One afternoon I was sitting in a beautiful city park and a man approached me, walking slowly along the winding pathway, a big Bible under his arm. He seemed to be going nowhere in particular and paused beside me for a moment, then sat down, and we began talking. When he told me where he was from, I was quite excited.

"I'm from the next village," I exclaimed, beaming.

"Then we're practically neighbors."

I was homesick and lonely after having been in the city for six months or so. Talking to someone from a town near my own village was almost like a visit from home. In the short space of half an hour or so, we became good friends, and when he told me what Jesus Christ had done in his life, I listened. Before he left, he invited me to attend his church the next Sunday. I thanked him, but I did not plan on doing as he asked.

Why should I go to some other church? I reasoned silently. *I am working under a church. If I go to any, I'll go there.*

For a long time I did not see my new friend, so he was not aware that his talk had transformed my life. Sitting in the park after he left, I got to thinking about my days in Hebrew school and my instruction for Bar Mitzvah. We had read in the Old Testament that our Messiah would come one day to be our King. In the New Testament I had read much about Christ who claimed to be the Messiah. I had to have it straight in my mind. I had to know whether Christ was our Savior or not. Was he the One Isaiah wrote about?

So I started going to church. Once I began to attend, some of the people started to call on me, but their visits did not keep me going—I went because I wanted to. I was interested in learning more about Jesus, who called himself the Christ. I also went because it was cold in my room on Sunday and it was warmer in the church.

Things were happening in my life, things I did not understand. I would think about the many times when I had been proofing type and had wondered, "What does this mean? Is Jesus the Messiah or not?" One afternoon I realized that Jesus Christ did fulfill the Old Testament prophecies, such as those in Isaiah 53:5: *"But he was wounded for our transgressions; he was bruised for our iniquities: the chastisement of our peace was upon him; and with his stripes we are healed."* I was so deeply moved, the tears flowed from my eyes.

I had many things to think through before I was ready to come face to face with this Christian faith. But I was on the way, one reluctant step following another. It was almost a year after my encounter with the Christian in the park—a year after I started to attend the church—that I turned to my Bible, determined to find answers.

At five o'clock one Saturday afternoon I began to read. Steadily I pored over the Word of God until eight o'clock the next morning, time for me to go to church. I was lost in the wonder of the statements I found in the Scriptures and the prophecies that tied the Old and the New Testaments together. Finally it all fit: my training in the Hebrew school, the Bar Mitzvah instruction classes, my questions as I typeset the New Testament.

I knelt and gave my heart to Jesus Christ.

No one was there to explain anything to me. No one told me how to pray. But the man with the Bible under his arm had pricked my heart in that brief time of talking and set it on the right path.

I finished praying, got to my feet, and hurried upstairs to the church. My life has never been the same since.

THREE   The First to Pray

SANDOR

I wanted to be baptized right away, but there was one man in the church who opposed it. Behind his back the people called him "soul killer" because he never wanted anyone to be baptized until a long time after they had received Christ.

"Wait," he told the congregation openly when I asked about going down into the water in baptism. "If he is only here to learn a business, he should not get baptized. If he has received Christ in his heart—if he is sincere—he will stay."

So they waited. I was just a little Jewish boy who had

no family in the church, so maybe they thought it did not matter if I was not baptized right away. I accepted their decision calmly. Perhaps they were right, I reasoned, putting my own wishes aside. Perhaps it was best if I was not impatient. I continued to go to services, and one and a half years later I was baptized, a happy day for me.

I went home a couple of times after I became a Christian. My family was happy to have me, but they were deeply disturbed that I had left the Jewish ways.

I did not tell them that I was a Christian at first, but they saw something different in my life. In the morning and at night I knelt to pray, just as I had in my room in the city. When they found out I had left the faith of our people, I was very much afraid.

"You should stay in the religion you were born into, Sandor," mama scolded. "It is not for you to be a Christian. Your parents are not Gentiles." That, to her, was the deciding factor. The Christian boys I had played with had been born into the Christian faith. It was all right for them to worship Christ. I was born a Jew, a member of God's chosen people. I should stay a Jew. I would see one day that the Messiah was still to come, just as Isaiah had prophesied.

"I cannot remain a Jew," I tried to explain. "Jesus Christ is my Savior. I walk with him."

Papa was sick in his heart when he knew that I had left the religion of my people, but he realized it was useless to talk to me. I would not change. Some Jewish fathers would have forgotten me as a son—or tried to. For many Orthodox Jews such as papa and mama, it was better to lose a child to death than to have him receive Jesus Christ. But not papa. He was soft in his love toward his children. Never could he have brought himself to say that I was no longer his blood, regardless of what I would do. Yet it was difficult for him, knowing that I had left the faith that meant so much to him and mama.

"Sandor," he said, a certain pleading in his voice, "do not tell anyone in the neighborhood that you are no longer Jewish by faith. Hide it from everyone while you are here."

That I agreed to do, because I knew the shame that would come to him if the other Jews learned that I was a believer in Christ.

Papa and mama did not disown me, but something between us was broken and things were never the same again. After two or three days, papa began suggesting that I should go back soon—very soon. "It is better you return to your place, Sandor," he told me sadly. "If you stay here, they might find you out."

I worked in the print shop for four more years until I learned my trade, and then two years after that. When the country was divided, part going to Czechoslovakia, Romania, Yugoslavia, and Austria, there remained only eight million people of more than twenty million in Hungary. It was not possible for the print shop to have enough business to keep it going, so I got a job as an apprentice in a tailor shop. However, the church was kept open, and I continued to go there. Two girls and I started going to the park, where we would gather the children together to sing songs and have a time for stories. When the children reached the place where they enjoyed it so much they wanted more, we took them to the church and started holding Sunday school for them.

There were not many ministers in Hungary at that time, only one hundred or so for more than six hundred churches. When it was known that I could preach, I was sent out to towns and villages around Budapest, to different churches every Sunday.

By this time I was earning a nice salary as a tailor and had been thinking it was time to marry. I was looking at the girls in the church, eighteen or more who came to our services regularly, with only three young men. It was difficult to choose so I decided, *Why not let God pick for me?*

A few weeks later, before one prayer meeting, the thought came, *The girl who is the first to pray loudly, this one you shall marry.* I didn't know why she would pray loudly. Even to this day I do not know, but that was the thought that came to me.

As usual, the preacher said a few words before coming to the part I had been waiting for. "Let us pray," he said. Everyone's head bowed. The first to begin praying was pretty Ester Schmidt, who prayed quite loudly that day. I was so excited I had a difficult time to keep from shouting.

ESTER

My mother stayed in the family home during World War I, while my father was held as a war prisoner by the Russians at a work camp in Siberia. Everyone said we would never see him again, that he would die in the cold, but mama was strong in her trust in God. "He allowed them to take him," she said firmly. "He will cause them to bring him back."

Papa did come home, exactly as mama had said he would. He was very sick from his stay in the mines, but slowly he got back his strength until he was able once more to work as a deacon in the church.

We moved to Yugoslavia after that. But this had become a big nation, and the Serbo-Croatian language became official and was taught in the schools. Papa spoke German and a little Hungarian. He did not know the new official language and in his heart he was a German, although the politicians told him he was now a citizen of Yugoslavia. Fortunately there were countless others like him, and many of the churches still used German for their services. Papa was eventually named the president of a German denomination in our new country. There were not too many congregations, but he had an important position.

I was fourteen when I felt that I wanted to belong to the church. I knew the songs and liked to sing them. I had always gone to Sunday school, and we had devotions every day in our home. I suppose you would say that I was taught everything I needed to know about receiving Christ as my Savior, but I only understood a little about salvation. Nevertheless, when they questioned me as to what I believed, I knew all the right answers. So I was accepted for baptism.

There was much the members of the congregation did not know about me at the time. They did not know that my lips spoke of my trusting Christ for salvation, but my heart did not grasp what they were saying. I remember feeling vaguely uneasy during the questioning, but when the vote was taken and I was accepted, the uneasiness passed. It was more than thirty years later that I learned the truth—that I had not personally accepted Jesus at the time I was baptized. Oh, I believed all I had heard about Jesus. I just did not have assurance in my heart that he had died for me.

I went back to Budapest a year before my family. I could only get a job teaching German to children, and many could find no work at all. Those days were hard. I had to work an entire month to buy a pair of shoes, and even then, there was not enough money to pay for them unless I lived on one or two meals a day.

The people in the church were very kind to me. My boss, who was a member there, gave me a room to live in and sometimes a meal, which was much for him to do. Life was hard for him, too, and he had little enough for his family.

It was not long after I moved to Budapest that Sandor asked God to show him who he should marry. I knew him, of course. Everyone in our church knew everyone else. He was slight of stature, but there was something about him that set him apart from the others, a spiritual quality that attracted me, although I did not understand it.

In 1928 we were married and our lives together began.

FOUR   A Tightening Noose

SANDOR

I was working as a tailor in Budapest, so we got an apartment in the city. I continued doing what I could in the church and Sunday school, helping with the young people and speaking to other congregations when I was asked.

There were certain things that bothered me about the church we were attending. For example, when the name of another Jewish believer came up for membership, a prominent member spoke against accepting him. "We already have three Jews who are members," he said, his face resolute. "That is enough." I expected someone to get up quickly and challenge him, but when the vote came our brother was rejected. It was not because they were uncertain about his testimony as a Christian. He had walked for a long while with the Lord. He was refused because he was a Jew.

I was also concerned because many of the church people loved Adolph Hitler. They were almost delirious with happiness when the Fuhrer sent his legions goose-stepping into Vienna. The Christians embraced each other gleefully and shouted, "*Heil* Hitler. *Heil* Hitler." Their acceptance of the Fuhrer was a sword in my heart, for I knew what he was going to do to the Jewish people in Germany. He had already told us exactly what we had to look forward to: *extermination!*

Once when I preached on the subject "The Jews—God's Chosen People," a university professor of stature who was also a church member, challenged me openly.

Those first years of our marriage were difficult for many people, but they were good years for us. I had a good job, and both Ester and I knew how to be frugal. Even after our daughter was born in 1930 we continued to save money. Three years later we bought a lot, as many others were doing, and built a house near Ester's parents, in a suburb outside Budapest.

At first we tried to continue going to the German church we had attended all of our married lives, but it was difficult to travel so far every Sunday. We did not even try to go to both the morning and evening services, but decided on going at night. We had to go into the city by train, a long ride, and out again after the meeting was over. It was particularly difficult for me, since I had to get up early on Monday morning to get to work.

"We should start going to the little church here in our own neighborhood, Ester," I finally suggested. "It would be so much easier than taking that long trip to the city every Sunday."

"But the services out here are in Hungarian," she protested, "and you know how much trouble I have with the language."

Actually, she did not have *that* much trouble with Hungarian, but German had been the tongue of her home. She had been taught to pray and read and sing in German. When someone spoke of a Bible verse, she thought of it at once in her parents' language, and then had to translate it into Hungarian.

I knew how hard she had tried to break through the barrier but little helped. It was boring for her to sit through a Hungarian service, but I kept asking anyway.

We began to drift in our spiritual lives, slowly, over a period of months, as our attendance at services became more and more sporadic. It was not long until we were only attending church on special occasions, or if we felt like it. A few months later we were so bored, we began to attend the movies at the local theater on Sunday afternoons.

I was not even aware of my spiritual drifting. One Sunday, we met three girls from the nearby church we had been attending occasionally in the lobby of the movie house. "Look, Sandor," Ester whispered in shame. "Young girls yet! And you are a preacher. What are we doing here? What sort of example are we to them?"

I did not answer, but I did not get much out of the film

that afternoon. Ester was right. I was still preaching occasionally and had to be an example. How could I tell others they should live for Christ when they knew I did some of the same things they were doing? When we got home, I told Ester, "We do not go there any more."

For a long while she sat on the sofa, staring intently at a picture on the wall. "I think it is better that we join the Hungarian church," she said at last. "It is not good that we do not go to services every Sunday."

This was what I had been waiting to hear her say. Together we joined the local congregation and began to take part in the activities there. It gave me new excitement in the Lord and helped in my preaching. I even seemed to have more love for the young people than before. For Ester, it was much different. She could speak Hungarian, but she didn't read the Bible in that language and could not pray in it.

When the minister of our little church took sick, I was asked to preach and did so every Sunday for as long as I was left at home. I was still preaching every Sunday when the Second World War broke out, and with it came the laws against the Jews. The happiness of our early married life was rapidly drawing to a close. I sensed this, but had no way of knowing the agony we were soon to experience.

ESTER

Although my papa was a deacon and had served in a high place in the church, he still trusted Hitler's promises.

"He will be good for Germany," papa said one day in a proud voice. "He will bring the country together and make us proud to be Germans again."

I could scarcely believe it was papa speaking. "That Hitler!" I exploded. "He wants to kill all the Jews. How can you be for him when you have such a good Christian son-in-law who is also a Jew?"

"God is permitting Hitler to take the control of our country away from the Jews," he protested.

Papa was as stern then as he used to be when he punished one of us children. His cheeks turned as red as the coals in the stove, and his voice got very loud. "You talk about Hitler as though he is some kind of animal, Ester. You are being deceived by the Jews. That is only their propaganda. He will put the Jew in his place, but he will not destroy him."

"It will happen, papa," I countered, as angry as he. "You wait and see."

When I came home from visiting my parents, I was sad and there was an ache in my heart. I did not want to tell Sandor what papa had said, but he pressed until I explained all that had happened.

"Your parents are Christians," he said. "Can you talk about the Bible with them?"

"Not now," I retorted, shaking my head. "Papa thinks only of Adolph Hitler and the glory he will bring back to Germany when he and his Nazis are in control."

"If you don't talk about the Bible and the things of God, Ester," Sandor said mildly, "don't go over there. It just makes trouble."

I found it difficult to understand my husband. Hitler was threatening to destroy his people. The hatred might even touch him, if that madman had his way. Yet there was no anger in his voice. "You can't do anything to change their minds, so don't talk to them about it."

After a while I began to understand a little of why my family was so pleased with the Fuhrer, as they themselves called him. "He put the men back to work," they said, "and gave purpose and direction to our nation when our people had been drifting in hopelessness and gloom."

But there was always the spectre of what was happening to the Jews. Already the storm troopers were beginning to herd Jews into concentration camps. Word appeared from time to time in our papers, and there were editorials all across Hungary lauding Hitler's courage and foresight in taking such strong action against a vile, untrustworthy people. A nation on the move, they wrote, could not afford to be vacillating and weak in such matters. I began to fear for Sandor, though he went about his activities as calmly as though all the world were friendly with the Jews.

Not long after that, it became apparent that Hitler was directing the policy of Hungary in such matters. Concentration camps were opened and arrests began. I tried once more to share my fears with papa and explain to him what sort of man this Adolph Hitler was.

"I don't know where you get your information, Ester," he said, "but it can't be true: Our leader is wise and decisive. He moves while other men think about what they should do. But he is not savage. He is not cruel. He is not forcing the Jews away from their homes into concentration camps. He would do nothing like that."

"Don't you see it, papa?" I exclaimed, anger making

my voice tremble. "Don't you read the papers? It is beginning to happen everywhere."

"*Nein!*" he shouted, as though I were a small girl caught fighting with a friend or my sister. "I will not listen to such talk, Ester! Not one more word!"

Then one afternoon he was going into the church he served when he saw the soldiers arrest a group of Jewish men and women in the street. They were not international bankers or wealthy industrialists exploiting the people. They were ordinary workers like ourselves, people with no money or position.

"There has to be some reason for what I saw happen today," he said defensively when he got home and told mama about it. "The Fuhrer would not do such things to common people unless they were enemies of the state." He got to his feet and paced nervously across the living room. "That's it! They were enemies of our country."

That helped to make him feel a little better, until a Jewish girl was shot and seriously wounded right in front of him. Other Jews had friends who would hide them, but not this girl. She was very poor and appeared to know no one well enough to ask for help. In desperation, one afternoon she went to the home of a Christian family not far from the church. Papa saw the door open to her knock, but not soon enough. Before she could slip inside, an officer came around the corner and fired at her, hitting her in the stomach at point-blank range. She screamed and cried out for help as she writhed on the steps. She would not die from her wound, but papa did not know that. When he came home, his face was pallid and his hands were trembling.

"I would never have believed it, mama," he said, his sadness evident. "What Ester has been telling me is true. The Fuhrer is killing the Jews." But his faith in Hitler was not completely shaken. "I still like him and his men. I just do not like his persecution of the Jews."

Papa never did tell me that he was wrong. His pride was too great for that.

SANDOR

When the war exploded around us, I became much more concerned about what might happen to me. Other Jews were taken to camps all over the country without even being allowed to tell anyone where they were going. One day it would happen to me too. I didn't know when or how, but I knew the day would come. By the time the war was a few months old, I received a draft call to go to a camp.

Ester and Ida watched mutely as I put on my coat and hat and left. I kissed them good-bye, but turned away quickly when my wife started to talk to me. Saying good-bye that day was as difficult as anything I had ever done. I didn't know if I would see them again in this life.

I went to one of the buildings in our village that had been taken over by the military, and a grim, granite-hard officer questioned me. "Name? Age? Nationality of parents? Nationality of wife?" He frowned when I told him I was married to a German girl.

"Jew?" he demanded.

"No, sir, she is not a Jew."

Then he wanted to know my religion.

"Christian," I answered.

He tapped the desk impatiently with his pencil. "How long?"

"Since I was sixteen years old."

His pencil poised over the form. "You can prove that?" he demanded.

"*Igen*," I answered, "yes. By the people in the church and my baptismal record. I was baptized before I was eighteen."

He made a notation on my paper. "There is a law that allows you to go free," he said. I thought I detected a certain reluctance in his voice. "If you became a Christian as a young man, you can be considered a Christian. Or if you are married to a Christian wife who does not have either parent Jewish and you belong to the Christian religion, you are not to be held. So there are two ways you could be freed." He dismissed me with a curt nod of his head.

Ester was astonished to see me when I returned home. "We prayed for you, Sandor," she cried. "A special service was called at church. We asked God to set you free, and now you come home to us!"

I took her in my arms and held her close as she sobbed her relief. But I was not deceived. I was free for a time, but the noose around me was drawing closer, and I did not know how to escape it.

FIVE   White Armbands

SANDOR

I tried to act as though nothing would happen to disturb
the quiet order of our lives, but I knew that my time at
home would not be long. The radio continued to pour
out its hate against the Jews, and many papers carried
the stories against us. I could not understand how
anyone would believe such terrible stories. If you
believed what was being published in the papers and
shouted on an increasing number of newscasts, Jews
were scarcely human.

I was not considered a Jew—the officer who
questioned me had said that. But even though this

provided a respite from the Nazi cages and work camps,
I found it disturbing. I was a Christian, but I was also a
Jew, a child of Abraham. My papa and mama were
Jews. Proud blood flowed through my veins, prouder by
far than that of any flaxen-haired Aryan.

I wanted to shout to a scorning, vengeful world that I,
too, was a Jew—and Jesus was a Jew. But I did not. I
had a wife and daughter to care for, and a group of
Christians who needed me to minister to them. So I
waited, knowing that each setting sun brought me
closer to the time when I would be snatched away,
scooped up in the same vicious net that was thinning
the ranks of my people.

I am not sure whether Ester realized what was soon to
happen or not, but I suspect that she did. If I was late in
coming home from work or was delayed in getting back
from a preaching engagement, I could read the terror in
her eyes. Neither of us mentioned it, but the spectre was
constantly with us.

I was spared for a time, but we knew that would only
be until the Fuhrer changed his mind and barked an
order to one of his generals. Or perhaps his mind was
already made up and the taking of Christian Jews like
myself was only another step in his diabolical plan of
extinction for my people.

It all happened swiftly. The Nazis moved into Hungary
to be greeted by cheering crowds, not as conquerors but
as returning heroes. No bombs were dropped, nor were
any guns fired in anger. Our nation seemed eager to be
taken over and made a part of Germany.

It was then that the blow fell. A new law said that if
anyone had a father and a mother who were Jews, he

must report to a work camp to help the war effort. It mattered not if he was a Christian or was married to a Gentile. If his parents were Jews, he belonged to the Jews. The announcement was well planned and timed. The day it was aired on the radio, it appeared in banner headlines in all the newspapers and on posters tacked up everywhere: ALL JEWS TO HELP WAR EFFORT. All Jews had to report to work camps immediately. No one would be spared.

ESTER

I was at the market when I first saw the posters saying that Sandor would be taken from Ida and me. Two slender, smooth-faced young men with hard eyes and the quick, confident movements of youth were nailing the dreaded announcement on lightpoles at every corner.

I stopped suddenly in the middle of the street, unmindful of the fact that bicycles and trucks and a huge crowd were surging around Ida and me. My trembling fingers sought our daughter's hand as I read the pronouncement. Ida was twelve years old at that time. I saw her as a slight, sensitive child who thought too deeply and had too much perception for one of her age. She felt the quivering of my moist fingers and looked up quickly, fear in her eyes.

"What is it, mama?" she asked.

I looked down at her, an icy aching in my heart. What was happening was going to be difficult enough for me, but it would shatter Ida's world. I had to spare her as much as possible. "It is all right," I told her, forcing strength and confidence into my voice.

She could read the poster as well as I could, and there was no mistaking the meaning. "Papa will be taken away, won't he?"

"*Igen*," I said. I could not lie to her. "He is going to help with the war."

Her voice faltered. "To be a soldier?"

"*Nem. Nem.* He is to work only."

She seemed relieved at that. "He will work in the city, won't he? He will be able to come home at night and stay with us." Her young features pleaded with me to assure her that it would be so. "Won't he, mama?" When I did not answer immediately, she repeated the question.

"I don't know. Perhaps they will have him work far away."

This she refused to accept. "No," she replied, "he will work like now and come home every night. If he does not, how can he go to the churches and tell the people about Jesus?"

I could not tell her that Hitler and his crowd were not particularly concerned about whether or not her father was able to preach.

When we reached home, Sandor had already gotten off work at the tailor shop and was in the living room. He tried to act as though nothing had happened. but we both knew that the end of our lives as a family had come, at least for a long while. His cheeks were pallid, and a quiet resignation deadened the sparkle of his eyes. In that moment I saw that he had been expecting this all along. I did not understand how he could be so calm and relaxed.

"Oh, Sandor!" I cried, fleeing to him. For the space of a minute or more we drew strength from the closeness of an embrace. Ida looked on somberly, stunned by this new development that she only half understood. I was sure I could not live through an entire day without my husband, but I wasn't reckoning on the strength that comes only from our God.

SANDOR

Now that the crisis was happening, a quiet peace took hold of me. No longer would my days be filled with uncertainty and dread as to when I would be taken. It had become a reality. Somehow this made the moment easier for me.

Not so with Ester. Her face was ashen and expressionless, and her hands, folded in her lap, were trembling. There were no tears, but her eyes were dull and suddenly sunken deep into her skull—or so they appeared, and an awful desolation marred her features. I was sure she would never smile again.

I wanted to take her in my arms once more and tell her that everything was going to be all right, that I would only be away for a few short weeks, but that would have been a lie. As far as I knew, I might never see either Ester or Ida again.

"You will make me the white armband, Ester?" I asked her. That also was a part of the law. Those who were Jews and worshiped as Jews had to wear the yellow Star of David, a symbol to all they met and talked to that they were a part of a despised people. The white armband that Jews like myself were to wear indicated that extenuating circumstances made us a little less contemptible.

But even the most ardent Hungarian Nazis did not know that we were being herded into camps for more than just labor. The masters of the Third Reich had launched their first pogrom against Jews who practiced their religion and lived as Jews, but they had long since decided that eventually *all* Jews were to be systematically destroyed. This we had feared from the very first, even though there had been no proof. Now they were moving against us, and we knew what would eventually happen.

The next morning, I reported to the school where I would be living with other Jews like myself. I was issued only a cap as a uniform and was shown the place where we would be living. It was a long, open room with straw thrown on the floor in place of a mattress. My nose picked up the strong odor of food being cooked in another part of the building. It did not smell like Ester's cooking but, like the place where we would be sleeping, it did not seem as bad as I had imagined. I had heard so many stories about the treatment of Jews in other work camps that I was surprised at what had been done to make us comfortable.

Ester and Ida came to the schoolhouse to see me as often as they could. They had to get there early so they could get back home before darkness took over Budapest and her suburbs. The entire area was under the most strict blackout. All homes and office buildings were tightly wrapped against leaking light. Cars, trucks, and streetcars operated without any sort of illumination, and the latter clanged from stop to stop in complete darkness. No one on the sidewalks knew whether they were crowded to capacity or empty.

The visit of my wife and daughter was the most memorable event of each week. In the morning when I would get up, my first thought was of them. *I wonder if Ester and Ida will come to see me tonight?* I even tried to guess how many hours it would be until I would see them. And when we left the factory at the close of the day, I was not thinking about the meal of thin soup or the chance to rest and let the hurt escape from my aching muscles. I was thinking about my family. They would soon be coming to see me. And when they appeared I was once more a new creature. We were separated, to be sure, and had no knowledge of what the future held, but we were one, a family unit that could not be torn apart.

I began to understand why God had given Ester to me. She was strong and steadfast and daring, while I was more cautious. She was determined to see that Ida's life was as normal and as free from tension and fear as possible.

Having to stay in the improvised camp and work in the factory dismantling machinery was a wearing experience for me. I was one of the smaller men in our unit, but was expected to do as much as anyone else. I would not have had it any other way, although I must confess that it was exceedingly difficult at times.

The food got progressively worse as the war lingered on. It was usually prepared of something smelly and totally undefinable, and the portions diminished so much that we were constantly hungry. A nagging resignation seized us. We would never be released, we reasoned, so it did not matter what happened to us.

I had not worked long when the American Air Force began to "visit" us with surprising regularity. How they determined that ours was a war plant, I have never been able to understand, but they knew. The planes would appear on the southern horizon, roar in, and dump their lethal loads on the entire industrial area.

The first time it happened, some of our work force bolted for the bomb shelters beneath the big buildings, but they were ruthlessly turned back by the armed guards.

"Those shelters are not for you. Go out there and wave to your American friends!" they shouted as they herded us out to the yard at one end of the building. "And see that you're still around when the raid is over!"

The doors were locked against us to keep us from sabotaging our tools. If our guards sought to make us angry at the Americans and frightened at the prospect of being killed, they had forgotten an important part of the human psyche. By holding us against our wills and systematically carting our Jewish brothers off to death camps they were depriving us of hope. And to a man who is hopeless already, what difference do bombs make?

We watched them come floating down. "There comes another," we said curiously and without emotion, "And another."

We were out in the yard at the beginning of one air raid when a younger man who worked with us, a tall, handsome Jew with a degree in engineering, boasted that he was not afraid. "I am a fatalist," he told us.

"Whatever comes will come. I don't need a crutch like Christianity."

He was still talking when a lad who was younger than he came hurrying up and whispered to him. I was close enough to hear him say, "Your wife is here! She was taken yesterday and is in a group that will walk to a death camp in Austria!"

The engineer's face blanched and tears leaped to his eyes. I looked up to see a motley crowd of Jews shuffling listlessly up the narrow street. The guards, upset at being caught out in the open during an air raid, were keeping an uneasy eye on the planes as they herded their prisoners around the corner.

The young man was so overcome he began to sob uncontrollably. He was unable to join us as we hurried out to the corner to see the ragged group.

Someone spotted his wife and motioned quickly for her to join us. She did so when the guards stepped around the corner and were out of sight momentarily. We opened our ranks, let her in, and closed so quickly the soldiers were unaware of what had happened. When they were gone, we took her to her husband.

"How did you do this?" he demanded incredulously.

The next day she took a train back to Budapest, where a Christian family hid her until the war was over and her husband was set free.

As the bombing increased in intensity we learned to judge where the falling missiles would strike. If it looked to be close, we threw ourselves flat on the ground. One day we saw a bomb dropping straight for us, and a scream of warning sounded from lip to lip. It came close to where we were lying, but made a direct hit on the underground bomb shelter that protected the Aryan workers in the factory and some of the families that lived nearby. Shrieks of terror drifted up from the subterranean chambers. Before we were back on our feet, an officer dashed up to assess the damage.

"Who are you?" he cried, staring at us. Miraculously not one of our number had even been injured.

We pointed to our white armbands.

"Come on!" he shouted. "Help get these people out!"

We set to work frantically clawing the dirt and broken pieces of concrete out of the way with our hands. A water main had broken, and the people in the shelter were standing shoulder-deep in water by the time we got down to them. Many of the children had already been drowned, but we were able to rescue many others. When the last person was taken from the bomb shelter and the last body retrieved we were sent back to our barracks for the rest of the day.

"I've been wondering something," the man next to me murmured. "If we had been down in that bomb shelter and they had been on the outside, how many of us do you suppose they would have dug out?"

SIX Aryan Hospitality

SANDOR

This second time I was in work camp, there was a
change in the guards' attitude. At first it was almost
indetectable, but as time wore on we began to see more
contempt in the way they acted toward us.

A cloud hung over the place where we were billeted.
The food became continually worse, and the prisoners
bickered and fought over little things. There had been a
certain amount of quarreling from the first, but it
increased as time dragged on. Bump into a man in line,
and he was apt to hit you with his fist or give you a shove
hard enough to send you sprawling. There were fights

in the morning when we got up, during the day when we were working, and at night when we had dragged ourselves, exhausted, back to the building where we were being held.

There was no way of predicting the guards' reactions to the fights. On some occasions they seemed to take savage delight in watching us brawl among ourselves and would do nothing to stop the trouble. On others it was an excuse for them to charge among us, rifle butts swinging, to restore order. "Dogs!" they would shout. "Stop it!"

It had never been a part of my nature to quarrel or fight—even when I was a child. To battle with my fellow Jews—men who were held by the same guards in the same work camp—was unthinkable.

"Look what we are letting them do," I would say. "They're making animals of us. When we squabble this way, we are giving them reason to say we're really not men."

A few listened, but most refused to hear what I was saying. The slightest irritation was enough to trigger an explosion at any time. I tried to keep to myself as much as possible, but I could not close my ears or eyes to what was going on. I did what I was told during the day, and at night I washed the clothes of the more wealthy internees to give Ester a little money.

The morning after Ester took my clothes home, December 8, 1944, I thought we would be going to work as usual, dismantling a factory to ship it to Germany. One factory after another was being stripped and sent west to help the war effort, the Hungarians who questioned it were told.

On this particular morning, however, we were not taken to the plant to continue our crating. Instead, we were marched to the railway station to be transported to Austria. We would be building tank traps against the storming hordes of Russians who were pressing relentlessly toward the heart of the Third Reich.

I thought about Ester and Ida. They would come in the afternoon with my warm clothes and a loaf of bread, only to find that I was gone and the building was emptied and locked. They would be worried that I had been taken to the gas chamber or shot, and there was no way I could get word to them that I was as well and strong as ever.

As we waited to be loaded into boxcars I prayed that God would give Ida strength during this time of uncertainty and danger. I prayed, too, for Ester. She was the strong one, but I knew that some of that was on the outside just to help Ida.

We were eighty-five or ninety people in one boxcar, jammed in so tightly we had to stand. We could not even lie down to sleep.

"How long?" one of the men close to me murmured.

"I heard a guard say where we're going," someone answered him. "It shouldn't take more than three or four hours. If we should happen to be on a very slow train, six at the most."

We could easily stand that I told myself. After working the way we'd been forced to, even being crowded was no problem.

Instead of a brief half-day of traveling, however, it took us an entire week. We hid on a siding during the daylight hours and crept forward at night, jouncing

miserably over the rough tracks. There were no
windows in the stifling cars, so we could not see out to
determine where we were. I often wondered if we had
spent the time going in circles, or if they kept us
traveling back and forth over the same tracks instead of
going directly to our destination.

We got no food or water during the entire trip. There
was not even an opportunity to go out to the toilet, so
there was nothing to do except to foul our clothes. The
stench became overpowering.

People died in our car, and I am sure in the others as
well. There were so many who were weak from the
grueling work and lack of food that they could not
withstand such physical punishment. When an
individual died, the body was supported upright by
those next to him. We were packed so tightly there was
no way the dead could be placed on the floor.

I found myself praying for those around me and for
myself, asking God to shorten our time of suffering.
However, it seemed as though he was ignoring our
misery. The hours stretched on endlessly, and there
was no relief for any of us.

Eventually, we reached the river at a point where it
separated Hungary from Austria. The doors to the cars
were opened, and we were told that we would be
addressed by a German officer before going into Austria
to work for the Fatherland.

While we waited, we saw long lines of Jewish men,
women, and children, surrounded by soldiers. They
were marched past the train to a field that hugged the
river. I could no longer see them, but could hear the
sharp, staccato commands in German.

Later some of the men who had been a little closer to the river told what had happened. I listened in horror as one of them said, "The soldiers took those prisoners out to the riverbank and formed a line of them. Then, twenty paces or so away, they also lined up. The officer gave an order and they shot everyone! Men and women fell backward into the river. You know how sluggish the water is there. The bodies floated slowly, and their blood stained the river red." He paused until he could speak again. "But that wasn't all! They brought in another group of fifty or more and did the same thing. Those who didn't die right away were allowed to struggle in their agony until they bled to death or drowned!"

"I was watching, too," someone else said, "and I feared for the man who stood next to me. He couldn't contain himself and muttered, 'Beasts! Beasts!' I prayed that he would not be overheard. Had a guard caught the words, there would have been one more added to the number of dead."

I tried to close my mind against what they were saying, but couldn't. *Dear God,* I prayed, *ease the pain for those who are about to be slaughtered. And somehow, God, stop this terrible thing that is taking place. Work in the hearts of the calm, smooth-cheeked young men who so callously and methodically go about the ugly business of exterminating innocent people whose only crime is that they have been born Jews.*

The army officer was late in coming to speak to us, but we had to remain standing until he came and had finished his brief message. He was tall and trim, a faultless specimen of Aryan perfection with blond hair and piercing blue eyes that seemed to be peering at us over vast arctic wastes. His personal contempt for us was obvious in the way he stared beyond us and in the icy tone in his voice. Still, he spoke quietly and in a tone that was almost gentle.

"Welcome," he began. "When you are in Austria, it is the same as though you were in Germany. We are very happy to have you here. You will get three meals a day. You will have a nice place to sleep. Everything will be all right for you."

We knew better than to put any trust in what he said. However, as soon as we were taken off the train and put in the camp, we were led to the dining hall where there was plenty of food for everyone. "If you don't get enough to eat the first time around," we were told, "come back and have some more. You have been six days without food. We don't want anyone to leave here without having enough to eat."

"I've never been so hungry," I heard a man say to his companion as I passed him, my own plate loaded with food.

"Maybe it is going to be better here than we thought," someone else observed. "If we're fed like this, it will be an easy place to work."

I went back twice more to get food. True to the officer's word, the soldier dishing out the meals gave me all I wanted. The only thing I noticed was that it was very salty. But when you have gone for six days without eating, you do not think about so small a matter.

"May I please have some water?" I asked.

His face grew cold. "Not now," he said.

"But—" I started to protest that I was burning with

thirst, but he cut me off savagely before I had an opportunity to finish.

"If you're done eating, go back to the building."

I remained motionless, uncomprehending for a moment or two what they were doing to us. There might be a shortage of food—that I could accept. But there was no shortage of water.

"Go on!" he exclaimed, his voice harsh and menacing. "You will get no water now!"

I realized slowly that he was in Hitler's elite guard, the SS troops. He could shoot me for not moving on; no one would question him for it.

Numbly I turned away, crossing the open area leading to the unheated barn near the Hungarian border. All 154 of us had been crowded into it since we first arrived at the camp. The salty food had every fiber of my body screaming for water.

I could see their plan now. They had kept us from eating for six days, until we were so hungry we would devour anything. Then they had fed us food that was loaded with salt. Now water was being denied us. I glanced about, bewildered. It was difficult to believe that fellow humans could be so cruel, regardless of how much they hated us.

The lack of water caused immediate problems. Some began to cry for it, their screams echoing and re-echoing through the drafty cow barn. Like many others, I fell unconscious, clutching frantically at my throat. In my agony I was sure that none of us would live through the experience.

Before I lost consciousness, however, one of the prisoners was shot, for no reason at all. Some time after

returning to the old hall, he had gone up to one of the
guards and asked to go outside to the toilet. The
arrogant young soldier did not answer him.

"I'm going out to the toilet," he repeated.

There was still no answer.

Taking silence for consent, he started for the door,
half out of his mind from lack of water. Once he stepped
outside, there was a rifle shot and he came staggering
back into the building, clutching his side.

A Jewish doctor sprang to help him. His hasty
examination revealed that the wounded man had to
have surgery at once. "This man must be operated on,"
the doctor told the officer in charge.

"*Nien!* No one leaves this building!"

"But he can be saved if we operate."

"*Nien!* He remains here!"

The poor man lay there screaming and writhing on
the floor. We all suffered with him through the night,
until he died. It seemed most difficult for the doctor who
knew he could have saved the man's life. How we prayed
that the poor fellow would die and end his suffering!

That long night was Christmas Eve, 1944, my first
Christmas away from Ester and Ida, and I cried.

SEVEN By the Grace of God

When the Nazis finally put us on a regular diet again, the food was much like that served to us in the school building in Budapest, only worse. There was a little bitter coffee in the morning. At noon we were given a bowl of weak soup, and at night a meal of potatoes cooked in their jackets and a few leeks. Both were boiled with the dirt of the fields still on them.

Some of the prisoners could not, at first, eat what we were being served. "I'd rather die than down that swill," they boasted. But they soon got hungry enough to come around to eating with the rest of us, ignoring the smells and the dirt.

I found it difficult to believe the cruelty of the men

guarding us. It seemed even worse than we had
experienced before. One of our number did something
one evening to offend the commanding officer. He
probably stole a little food or lost his temper and cursed
one of our captors. Surely his indiscretion was
deserving of no more punishment than a warning or the
taking away of privileges. But this was Nazi Germany
and he was a Jew.

"Put him in the river," the officer ordered.

The soldier hesitated. We were in the middle of a bitter
winter, and I am sure the guard was thinking of the
suffering the man would have to endure.

I happened to be close enough to hear the guard say, "I
could shoot him, sir."

The officer's cheeks reddened at such
insubordination. "Put him in the river! I want to see
how long it takes a Jew to die!"

The internee was prodded out to the stream at the end
of a rifle and forced to jump in, while the officers stood
on the bank, warm and comfortable in his great coat,
taking sadistic pleasure in his victim's agony. Soon he
tired of the sport and went to his barracks to sit by the
fire, but his order stood.

The water was cold, but not cold enough to take the
unfortunate man's life quickly. For he had to suffer in
the water. It became dark. On two or three occasions we
saw the officer in charge of us stride confidently to the
river's edge, to see how his prisoner was doing.

Inside, none of us even mentioned the terrible thing
that was happening outside. At least I heard no
comments about it, but it had its effect on all of us.
Stark anger mingled with the terror in our eyes, and our

gray, wasted faces tensed with fear. We could see once more that there was no hope for any of us. If we weren't killed tonight, it would be tomorrow or the next day or the next. There didn't have to be a reason for it. Just being there at the wrong time could be enough to incur the wrath of one of the officers. And that could be enough to cause us to suffer the same fate as that man whom we never saw again.

It didn't even have to be the commanding officer we displeased. For that matter, it didn't have to be an officer at all. Any guard could kill any one of us at any time, with or without reason, and without fear of punishment or even a reprimand.

For a week or more after the prisoner was killed, a cloud hung over the camp, a thick, oppressive curtain that robbed most of us of the hope that we might live to be released.

I felt the same concern, the same fear as anyone else. And I went through the same long, desolate nights of loneliness. I would have been less than human if I had not. But increasingly I experienced a great sense of peace and God's keeping power. I could feel his presence with me when we had been working such long hours that I quivered with exhaustion. I could feel his nearness when I lay alone in my bunk, concerned about Ester and Ida, knowing they felt the same loneliness and periods of despair that threated to overwhelm me. There was a calmness, a quietness of heart that I could not explain. Even today I do not understand the serenity, the joy in Christ that was mine, except that it was the gift of our loving God.

I maintained a brief period when I would be alone

with God every evening, which was a practice I had started when I was a sixteen-year-old lad and have continued until this day. Because of the noise and confusion in the cow barn at night, I made a practice of going outside to be alone when I prayed.

One of the first nights after we arrived, I was outside the building when a young SS trooper approached me, speaking softly in Hungarian. "I've been watching you," he said. "You come out here to pray, don't you?"

I nodded, wondering what would happen next.

"I'm a Christian, too," he almost whispered. "God bless you!" Then, lest he be seen fraternizing with a hated Jew, he turned away.

During the days and weeks that followed, I watched that young man. He was different than the others. Everyone noticed. There was no arrogance in his manner and he was kind, while his fellow guards were ruthless and savage.

Not long after the man was put into the river, I went out to pray as I always did. Two SS guards approached me. Although it was quite dark, I could see the revolver in the hand of one of them. He swore angrily at me, and in that instant I knew I was going to be shot.

"Don't shoot! Don't shoot!" a familiar voice cried out in German. It was that of the Christian. But his companion was not to be stopped.

"O God," I prayed silently, "I am ready to die. Take my spirit!"

There was a loud, metallic click as the soldier squeezed the trigger, but the gun did not fire. Cursing bitterly, he tried again. Still nothing happened.

"Don't shoot him!" the Christian shouted in

desperation. "Don't do this!"

There was a third sharp sound of metal against metal, but the bullet did not fire. This time the younger soldier had thrown his arms about the one who was determined to kill me and pulled the man away.

"Don't do this! He's only standing there praying. He isn't doing anything!"

I stared numbly into the darkness, finding it difficult to realize exactly how close to death I had come.

A friend heard the commotion and came out. "What's happening?" he asked.

I turned to my friend. "We'd better go back in."

Once inside I told him what had taken place. And ended with the statement, "God caused the pistol to misfire."

I saw doubt cloud his eyes.

"Three times," I added.

"That can't be!"

"Not only that, but he placed a Christian soldier there to stop the man who was determined to kill me."

My friend, Aaron, shook his head. "If anyone else had told me that, Sandor, I'm not sure I would have believed it."

That night I found it hard to get to sleep. In a new way I realized how much God loves his children and how closely he watches over and cares for us. I think he must have had a special reason for permitting me to see the extent of his marvelous loving-kindness. He knew what was in store for me and wanted to prepare me for it. However, at the time I only knew what had happened that evening. Mercifully the future was withheld from me. I thanked and praised him for his care and

thoughtful protection as I lived day by day, hour by
hour, minute by minute.

The commanding officer in charge of our camp was a
cruel, heartless man. Many times we had to work very
hard and didn't get more food. Many of our number got
so weak, they were not able to work the way we were
expected to. When anyone lagged behind, the guards
were ordered to beat them, a task in which they seemed
to delight.

It hurt me to see old men and women, or those whose
bodies had been broken under the savagery of the
soldiers, beaten when they were working as hard and as
fast as they could. At the same time, it seemed as
though God had made it possible for me to have more
food, so I was stronger than the others. I was better able
to withstand the beatings than some. It was just
possible that I might be able to save the lives of two or
three if I could convince the guard to beat me instead of
them.

When I first considered this, the strength fled from
my slight frame. I didn't consider myself a hero, nor a
martyr. But as I prayed, God seemed to be telling me
that this was what he wanted me to do.

Reluctantly I went to the officer the next morning. "I
am stronger than the others," I explained. "When they
can't work, hit me."

His eyes narrowed. "You mean that?"

"I do."

The guard acted as though he was about to refuse.
Then he shrugged his shoulders indifferently. "If that's
what you want, we'll try it that way."

I could tell by his tone that he thought I was out of my mind and would soon be pleading with him to stop. But I did not, and only God can be praised for that. At times I felt as though I could not take another blow, but the Lord always gave me the strength to spare some of my weaker brothers.

I also tried to help my friends in other ways. I would work as fast as I could to get my work finished so I would have time to help some of the slower ones. That spared me a beating as well.

Every morning they got us up at five o'clock and would have us standing at attention in the chill morning air until they were ready to give us a cup of warm black coffee and a piece of bread made with sawdust filler. We had to be in the fields ready to work at seven o'clock. It took an hour to get there, so we had to leave by six to walk to where we were digging the tank traps. We dug ditches without anything more to eat until lunch time. Then we were given some potato soup made from unpeeled and unwashed potatoes.

As the war continued, the bombings increased. Even the Russians were sending over a few planes, but their raids were feeble compared to those of the Americans. The bombers from the States roared in as thick as locusts, and when they left, the city and factories were burning.

After one intense air raid that sent flames and smoke billowing skyward, a Nazi officer called our people together for a special job. "I want twenty-four of you to go to work now," he said. Looking over the entire group, he chose the ones he wanted; I was among them. "I want you men to go to the railroad tracks where the trains are burning, and rescue what you can. You can eat what you want to eat and take what you want."

We went to the tracks and set to work, not caring for our lives. It mattered little to us whether we lived or died. After all, death would at least end our suffering.

Quickly we rushed close to the burning cars, opened the couplings, and separated those on fire from the rest of the train. How many people we saved that day I do not know, but there were many. When we finally finished our task, we dropped, exhausted, to the cold ground.

We expected nothing from the officer. Usually they told us what would help *them* for the moment, only to do as they pleased later. This man, however, was different. He had one of the cars opened and invited us to help ourselves.

"You did a good job," he said. "Take what you wish."

We ate, first—great quantities of cheeses and bread, until our stomachs could hold no more. Then we began to help ourselves. Like the others, I made a basket with the front of my shirt and began to fill it with soap and matches and candles. It was our experience that if we were taken to the countryside, which often happened, we would be able to trade such things to farmers for food. I filled my shirt with things I thought I could dispose of easily and secured the load by tightening the drawstring at the bottom. A young prisoner came over to me just as I was finishing. Although there were several others close by, he spoke only to me.

"Don't do as everyone else is doing," he said quietly. "Don't take matches and soap and salt. Take food this time."

It seemed strange that he would single me out among

all the workers, and even more strange that I would do as he said. Insofar as I knew he wasn't even a Christian. Why would God send such a one to speak to me? All I knew was that even as he spoke, I realized that God was using him. It is so unreasonable I had to think of it as a minor miracle. The instant he finished speaking, I opened the string and everything fell out. Then the two of us collected as much food as we could while everyone else took all the staples they could carry.

One of the men chided me about it. "I see you are not a good Jew," he retorted. "You are a stupid converted Jew because you do this. You watch! We will get much more food by trading with the farmers than you will have this way."

"That is all right," I said to him. "I will leave you with what you have. You leave me with what I have."

Less than three days later, we were awakened at two o'clock in the morning and ordered to start walking. We were given nothing to eat. We all gathered up as much of our cache of supplies as we could before we left. The others had soap, salt, matches, and candles. My young friend and I had bread and cheese.

We left the town in the dark of the winter night and walked in ragged lines along the back roads. There were farmers in the area, but that was of no help to any of us. We were prodded forward whenever we began to slow our pace. There was no opportunity for anyone to bargain with the farmers or their wives.

Hour after long, miserable hour we walked, until our feet were like lead and our very beings trembled with fatigue. Still, we had to keep on the move. They would not allow us to stop, and if we stumbled and fell we would be shot without warning.

As we were walking, I saw the man who laughed and called me a stupid Jew. He was so hungry he had started eating soap.

"What are you doing?" I asked him.

"I must eat."

"Don't do that," I told him. "Come over here and I'll give you some bread and cheese."

His gaze raised to meet mine, belligerently. I don't know whether it was because the hunger was stealing his reason, or if he disliked me so much he could not bring himself to let me help him. Whatever the reason, he refused.

"I don't need it," he retorted angrily, as though I had insulted him by offering him food.

Later that same day I saw him stumble and fall, frothing at the mouth from the soap he had been devouring. The guard shot him where he lay, not even giving him the opportunity to get to his feet again.

My heart ached for him. I could have fallen beside that poor man, the victim of my own mistake, had it not been for God's guidance.

I shared the food I had taken with me and ran out before the march was over. A German soldier I had never met before gave me something to eat, and a woman who was watching us march past her farm home came out and slipped five or six small loaves of bread to me. She gave bread to some of the others, too, but the soldiers saw her and took it away from them. I alone was able to hide it among my clothes before the Germans saw me. On the entire march there was not a day that I had to go without food.

EIGHT "How Do You Want to Die?"

Every day seemed to give them new ways of torturing us. At first we were working with the shovel on tank traps, digging holes so deep they would stop the Russian tanks. But the procedure did little more than slow the Russian armored units. Even so the Nazis kept us digging traps until there was no land left to hold them.

Then we were made to walk. But not to get somewhere. That we could have understood. Instead, we just walked to the Danube River and back, with guards to keep us moving and to shoot those who could keep going no longer and fell. Never did they give us anything to eat. I think they did not even like it when the people who lived along the road gave us food, but they did not forbid it.

"They can't," the man walking next to me explained. "International law requires that they permit people to give food to prisoners of war."

I don't know whether that was right or not. The Germans never seemed to be bothered by breaking any kind of law; but whatever the reason, they let us eat the food Austrian farmers gave us. Their selfless sharing saved the lives of many.

"But for what?" some of the prisoners asked bitterly. To walk and walk and walk again, until the senses were numbed and the body screamed for relief. To walk until death was the friend, and life the enemy.

Always the walking ended back at the cattle barn, until one night when we were routed from our beds and forced to walk. That had happened before, but this time we were not to come back. We marched to the river in a cold, drizzling winter rain that caused some to come down with pneumonia. Still, we had to stay out in it for two long days, shivering. None of us got to eat during that time.

It was then that I learned to eat grass as a source of food and strength. I don't remember whether I saw another prisoner doing it, or if I tried it in desperation. Whatever the reason, I soon found that it was good—far better than the horrible mixture the Germans fed us. And fortunately we were marching along roads that were lined with grass. It was simple enough to reach out and grab a handful on the way. There was nourishment in it, and it made no one sick. With a little water and plenty of grass, most of us could keep our strength.

Of course the Nazis didn't allow us to eat grass. At times soldiers were stationed where they could shoot if they saw us move out of line to get grass. On one occasion I was shot at. Whether the soldier intended to hit me or deliberately missed, I do not know. But he only fired once. I had been spared by God's grace, but I was so numb and uncaring I scarcely noticed.

We didn't know where we were being taken or what would happen to us. But at last the boat came to take us to a camp at Mauthausen in the mountains of northeastern Austria. We were crowded below decks in the clumsy riverboat, just as we had been in the cattle cars on the train from Budapest. It was only half-a-day's journey at normal speed, but the Nazis stretched it out to last for ten days. There was no food for us on the entire trip, and only a little water.

For many of the weaker ones, the ordeal proved too savage to withstand. People died where they lay, and again it was not possible to remove the bodies. We could only look past them, trying to pretend they were not there. But one cannot ignore death.

We were beyond crying, but we did mourn. There was a deep ache in our hearts as another succumbed to the artificial rigors of a trip that could have been easy.

I kept wondering why I should be spared and not the one whose body lay a few feet away. Surely God loved him as much as he loved me. There was no answer. Just that looming question, and one other. Would I be next?

At last the boat reached Mauthausen and stood a few feet off shore, straining at her lines. A long plank six- or eight-inches wide was put down from the deck to the bank, and we were ordered to walk across it. Soldiers were on either side, rifles ready to shoot the ones unfortunate or unsteady enough to fall into the river.

As the first prisoners started forward, weak and staggering from a lack of food and water, the officer in charge shouted a command. "Run! Run!"

We had to run up the passageway, across the deck, and down the narrow gangplank. From where I was standing, I could not see when someone fell. But I didn't have to. The dreaded report of a rifle signaled the fact that one of our number was dead. Another body would be drifting slowly downstream. How many lost their lives during that unloading process I do not know. I started to count the shots, but could not continue.

Each bullet is a life snuffed out, I told myself in agony. *I can't keep record, as though I'm keeping score in some game.*

When it came my turn, I breathed a quick prayer and started to run. I crossed as nimbly as though I was half my age and strong and well.

"Thank you, God," I murmured in a voice little more than a whisper.

I had not been on the riverbank long when a fellow internee who had just come off the boat approached me. Only the day before he had been boasting that he was an atheist! I can still hear his arrogant voice: "I don't care what you say or how many Bible verses you quote to me, you'll never get me to change my mind. *There is no God!*"

Now he stood before me, his gaunt, emaciated face taut with emotion. His cheeks were flushed as though from fever, and his very being trembled with fatigue.

"I'm so sick and weak I can hardly walk three steps

without staggering," he said. "I was sure that I would be one to fall in the river and be killed. Just before I was to go, I asked God to help me. I don't know why I prayed, except that I was sure I couldn't make it across the plank and was so desperate I had to turn somewhere for help. And he helped me, Sandor. I ran across that plank like a twenty year old. Now I *know* there is a God!"

I saw him frequently during the next few weeks and had a number of occasions to talk with him about our Savior. There was a change in his life that everyone noticed. I had another brother in Christ.

Once we left the boat, we hoped we would be able to lie down and rest. We were so bone-weary from lack of food and water and the exhaustion of the tortuous trip we thought it impossible to move another step. Yet we had to walk farther to reach the camp. We weren't told how many kilometers, or if it would mean another miserable night. All we knew was that we were being prodded forward callously. The soldiers were still with us, marching at either side, their powerful rifles ready to fire. Let one of our pitiful line falter and a bullet would keep him from getting up again. If he was too weak to walk without stumbling, he would be unable to work. And if he couldn't work, of what use was he? they reasoned.

Many died in the ditches or along the side of the road. And we dared not stop to help them, or see if they were friends. I staggered on, almost blind from weariness, concentrating each moment on placing one foot in front of the other and on keeping my balance.

A friend not far from me was having even more difficulty. He was so worn out and ill, he would catch a toe on a small rock or a clump of dirt and sprawl forward on the hard ground. While we watched and waited fearfully, expecting the sound of a shot, he would scramble upright once more and stagger on. His body was sapped of strength—of everything except a fierce desire to live. Fifty or a hundred paces farther along the road he would fall again, this time on the other side. Yet he would get up before a soldier could fire, and force himself to resume his place in the ragged, misery-choked line. He had such a fierce will to live he would not quit.

I learned much about determination and the power of the human mind over the body from him. He would not allow himself to be beaten by circumstances and somehow he managed to survive.

Fortunately for all of us the camp at Mauthausen was not far away. We reached it that night and were given water, a little food, and an opportunity to rest. The next morning and for as long as we were held there, we had to stand at attention for two hours at a time. Those who were too tired and weak to do so were shot as they fell to the ground.

It was not necessary for the Nazis to force us to stand as they did. It was not to help their war effort, but to cause us to fall from weakness so we would be destroyed. Why they had to put us through such torture I will never know. We were completely in their power. They could have killed all of us, or as many as they wanted to, each day without making us suffer. Still, it seemed as though they had to make a reason for our deaths.

I was sure my time would come while I was being held

at this camp. I was not a fatalist, but I was positive I would be shot here at Mauthausen. I did not look at death with dread, nor did I anticipate it as release. I was too weary, too wasted from the lack of food and water and the constant fear and hopelessness, to care what happened to me.

There was much rain at that time, and the camp yard was soupy with mud and water. We saw many prisoners fall into the mud, face down, and suffocate or drown because they were too weak to get up or turn their heads. And we had to watch them die. We were too near collapse ourselves to have the strength to help them. We tried, but our quivering, emaciated bodies would not respond.

A prisoner I had not seen before asked me to get some bread for him from the group of Yugoslavian women who were baking nearby. "You speak German," he told me. "Take this wedding ring and trade it for bread."

To have a gold ring of any kind was a crime punishable by death, but I did not think of that. We all broke such laws many times. I got the bread for him, thinking no more about it. I had done such things many times to help others.

I should have realized something was wrong when I no longer saw him around the camp. However, it was not until I was called before a senior officer that I knew the Nazis had brought in an informer. On the desk in front of the towering German was a revolver, a heavy club, and the ring.

"You sold this ring," he said coldly.

I did not answer. He was not asking me, he was telling me. Not that it would have mattered. He was judge, jury, prosecuting and defense attorneys, and executioner.

"Because you have done this, you must die. But since you are a good man, you may chose your death. Shall I shoot you or hit you with this stick?"

In silence I prayed. My mind told me to choose the gun. Any thinking person would do so: such a death would be quick and sure and the pain would not be as great. But when I spoke, that is not what I said. "I want to die with the stick," I told him.

I think it was a surprise to the officer. It was to me. Even now I can establish no logical reason for it.

The officer ordered me to stand up. I did so and saw him lift the club. I remember only a sickening blow to the head, but I must have fallen out of the doorway onto the cold ground. I was unconscious and nobody cared about me any more. Night came, and they went back to their barracks, leaving me alone. The Nazis didn't even come back to check whether I lived or died.

At some time during the night I woke up and dragged myself back with the others. God had spared me from certain death, but I was sure I could not stand another minute of the excruciating pain I was suffering. I am quite sure I had a concussion. Although I was too ill to realize what had happened, I was dimly aware that God had guided me to choose a beating rather than the bullet.

The next morning when we were called to stand at attention, I got up and staggered out with the rest. I was in such pain I didn't think I could make it through the first fifteen minutes. But at the end of two hours I was still standing there. I had again been delivered. For what, I did not know. It was not because of any worth in me. I can only conclude that my work on earth was not yet over.

By this time the war was not going well for Gemany. The Allies had opened a second front on "Omaha Beach" in France across the channel from England, and American bombers were roaming the Third Reich at will. Troops had poured across France and parts of Germany. Although German soldiers and civilians alike were telling themselves that soon new rockets would be blasting the Allies and turning them back to the sea, they were drawing so close to Mauthausen that the Nazis moved us again, farther into the interior.

We walked for five or six days without food. I don't know why they stopped us where they did. It was not to give us rest, of that I am positive. In the eyes of the Nazis we were not men. We were only animals, a little lower than pigs.

An officer spoke, "At this time everybody can eat good food and as much as he wants." We had to stay in line to get some warm soup. But the soup had such a terrible odor there was no doubt it was spoiled. Still we ate greedily. Many got very sick and could not walk and those who fell to the ground were shot by the guards.

By this time I was insensible to pain, stupefied by the relentless scourging of the soldiers who guarded us. I moved as one in a dream, step by reluctant step. Since I had been struck on the head, it was as though the little desire to live had been squeezed out of me. I was acutely aware of the suffering around me, but my own feelings were blunted. The fact that I was suffering from hunger and thirst and the bitter, driving cold did not register.

NINE Death Camp

We only stopped for a short time at Wells before starting
to the death camp that was to be our final destination. It
was one of those places that swallowed up the Jews of
Eastern Europe. People went in alive, but no one came
out. Hitler had these camps in mind when he said,
toward the end of the war, "We do not know how the war
will come out, but it is certain the Jews will cry."

The officers in charge of our wretched group took
sadistic delight in telling us where we were going. "This
time," I heard a guard say, "you're not going to be sent to
a place where you'll be treated so good. They've finally
decided that even Christian Jews are like the rest.
There's no use trying to rehabilitate you."

We didn't answer him, but we talked about his remark in tense whispers. "You know what that means," a friend told us. We nodded: the gas chambers or the firing squad, or simply being worked until all strength was gone and we would fall to the ground, unable to get up before we were shot.

"What difference does it make where they take us?" someone asked. "The death camps are all alike."

"Not quite," someone else ventured. "One camp can be much harder than another. It depends on the commanding officer. If he is cruel, he treats the people that way. If he is not so cruel, he treats them better."

"But the end result is always the same—the extermination of the Jews."

We knew of Auschwitz and Dachau and a few of the more notorious camps. We heard stories about them, how the people were forced to dig their own graves before being killed. We were aware that such a fate awaited us. Death was coming. Indeed, it was just outside the door, awaiting the caprice of the monsters who held us.

I rebelled inwardly as I saw another group of men and women, whose armbands identified them as Jews, working just outside one city we passed. Although they were guarded by a large detachment of soldiers, I talked to them as we walked by.

"What are you doing?"

They looked queerly at me, as though there had to be something wrong with me to ask such a foolish question. I should have been able to see, their eyes told me.

"We are working here."

"Do you get anything to eat?"

"*Igen*," they told me. "We eat. It is not good food, but we get plenty of it."

I stared at them, envy gnawing at my heart. Their cheeks were full and their arms strong and muscular. It was obvious that they were getting enough food. I was more jealous of that group than I had ever been of anyone in my entire life.

It would be nice to be able to work and to eat when I was hungry. Why could I not stay with them? I asked myself bitterly. Why would God allow me to be treated so cruelly? Why was I being taken to a place that would mean certain death?

I cried out to God, but there was no answer. I felt deserted by him. It seemed as though he had turned his back on me. Deep within, I knew that was not true, but my pain was so fierce I could not reason.

As I walked, I began to consider the suffering of Jesus Christ on the cross. He did not have to die there. He did it for me, Sandor Berger, so I could have victory over death and spend eternity with him. Who was I to expect to be treated differently than any other Jew? God would not allow me to suffer any more pain than I was able to bear.

After a tortuous march that ended much too soon, we reached the death camp. The village nearby was very similar to any other town in that part of Austria, a cluster of houses and shops squeezed together on a clearing hacked out of the forest by past generations. It was a beautiful old town, with narrow streets that bristled with buildings as sturdy and as indestructible as the farmers who tilled the hard, unyielding soil in the fields. Visitors today would call it quaint, but on that day we saw none of its beauty and charm.

There were no cars on the cobblestone paths that served the city as streets, and only a few old bicycles. People were plodding along the walks, bent on errands known only to themselves, but most surely in some way connected with eking out their miserable existence. I could not help noticing the scarcity of men. We saw the very old, leaning heavily on their canes as they hobbled along the sidewalk, and the very young, skipping with carefree abandon. But the work force, the heart of the village, was gone, ripped away to help move the Nazi war machine. The places of the men in the village had been taken by the women, grim-faced and sorrowing, women worn down by being forced to the tasks of men, women who had been stripped of their hope.

They knew who we were, where we were going, and what was going to happen to us. In their own misery, I am sure they felt compassion for us. Although we were being held captives by their leaders, we were kindred spirits, the victims of the same war.

They would look at us only to turn quickly away if our eyes met theirs. They seemed ashamed, somehow, at our being aware that they were staring at us.

Occasionally we would see a gray-haired woman, wrapped in peasant black, stop and cross herself. Although I was not Catholic, I found the act comforting. I liked to think that she was praying for us. And I prayed for her, too, as we went on down the street.

We left the outskirts of the village and approached the camp. I don't know what I had expected, but it was far less forbidding than I would have imagined a death camp to be. It stood by itself in the forest clearing, far from any farmhouses or woodcutters' dwellings. The buildings were low and rambling, stark gray objects built of weathering, unpainted wood. They were enclosed by a high fence with electric wires at the top and bottom, formidable deterrents for anyone foolish enough to attempt an escape. But the Nazis did not depend on the fence and high voltage wires alone. They also had soldiers with their trained dogs patrolling the outer perimeter, dogs as vicious as their human masters.

There were 17,000 of us at the camp, crowded into the facilities prepared for half the number. Not that the crowding mattered. Each passing day there was a little more space for those of us who were left. The methodical, logistically minded Nazis had put their slide rules to work and decided they could dispose of 400 bodies a day.

Before the prisoners got to go back to their barracks each day, a count of bodies was taken. If 400 had died that day, everyone else was returned to the barracks. If the number of deaths was short, the guards fired indiscriminately until they had 400 bodies for the burial details the next day. The Nazis were very efficient about such things. Our numbers would have quickly been decimated if the Germans had not been continually bringing in other contingents of Jews.

On some occasions we were given soup once a day. It was a horrible mixture that could scarcely be called food. Several times some who ate it died of food poisoning. Still, we were so hungry we forced ourselves to eat every drop that was given us.

I will never forget the day I went out into the yard to get grass to eat and met another man who had come out to trade for some potatoes. He had some bread and was trying to locate someone who would give him potatoes for a loaf of it. He stopped a few paces from me. I had seen him before, I was sure. There was something about his thin, emaciated frame and starvation-sharpened features that was familiar. His skin had an ashen hue of fatigue that marked him as one of us, and his eyes were deep-set and ringed with shadows. He had come shuffling listlessly across the exercise yard in my direction. A few feet away he stopped. I did not recognize him at first and he did not recognize me, although I could see that he was searching for my name in the inner reaches of his mind. Then his eyes lighted.

"You are Sandor!" he exclaimed brokenly.

It was my brother from Romania. Romania had not given over their Jews to the Nazis, but there had been a short time when part of that country was made a part of Hungary again. It was just long enough for all of the Jews and most of my family to be taken.

We threw our arms about each other and wept.

My brother's story tore at my heart. He and his family had been held for a time in Auschwitz. There he had seen his wife and two children taken into the gas chamber and killed. He had been spared because he was a skilled auto mechanic, and the Nazis needed him desperately. But now that they had finished with him, they had sent him to die with the rest of us.

Not all of the German soldiers were cruel to us, even while we were being held in the death camp. I remember an officer who came among us with sandwiches hidden somewhere on his person. When he was alone with us, he would slip a sandwich from the pocket of his heavy overcoat or a hiding place under his shirt and give it to us. It was a terrible risk he took; it could have meant prison or even death for him if he were caught.

I had been in the death camp for three weeks when the end came. The morning began as usual, with our guards firing among us to kill the quota of 400. There was a grim order in all that they did, even to the last hour they held the camp.

We were still standing there, that awful sickness churning in our stomachs, when there was a rifle shot outside the building.

I heard it. I distinctly remember that. But at first it didn't register that it was any different than any of the other rifle shots we were accustomed to hearing. I had been suffering from boils because of the poor food we were given, and had just had them opened with a razor blade by one of the Jewish doctors. The ailment was a common one and the doctor, a well-known surgeon, had asked for a room and a table for the operations and some medicine and cottom. Characteristically the Nazi officers had refused. So he was forced to open the boils with razor blades and clean them up without soap-washed rags. The incidence of infection under such conditions was high, but it was better than allowing them to rupture and clean themselves. The pain I felt as I stood there was terrible, yet I felt better, if that is believable, for I knew the worst of that illness was over.

Suddenly the Nazis stopped firing among us. At that moment I remember wondering what had been different about that earlier rifle shot. Outside, all sound was swallowed up by the roaring of engines as American and German fighter planes fought almost directly above. Then came the deathlike hush that occasionally comes before a major event.

During that period, the German troops disappeared. Some of the men and officers fled. Others had hidden civilian clothes in the building and changed hurriedly, concealing their uniforms and mingling with us as internees. Most of our number were not aware of that. We only knew that the soldiers were no longer in sight.

For half an hour or so we milled aimlessly about, like cattle, expecting something to happen but not knowing what. We had temporarily lost the ability to think and act for ourselves. I don't know about the others, but I feared that this was another German trick, that they would be waiting for us, machineguns at the ready, if we tried to leave the building.

After a time, when we were beginning to wonder if we dared go outside, other soldiers appeared. They came suddenly, brandishing their rifles. They were as young and as smooth-cheeked as the Germans, but there was a difference that I could not understand—an exuberance in their manner, a boyish excitement. I suppose it was the joy of being able to liberate us.

We had learned, in some small way, to cope with the grim cruelty and efficiency of the Nazis. This was a new dimension, and because we could not understand it, we were afraid. But we could tell at a glance that they were another nationality; their uniforms were different, for one thing. But we didn't realize they were Americans.

While we wondered what was going to happen, a voice

in Hungarian sounded above the melee. "Everyone
gather together and be quiet! You are to hear a speech in
Hungarian!"

An order. Our Nazi masters had trained us to follow
orders. Dutifully, we fell silent. In the hush of the
moment a soldier—to this day I do not know if he was an
officer or an enlisted man—climbed up on something
high so we could all see him.

"Now you are free!" he shouted. "You are all free! The
American army has taken this camp. You will be
required to stay here until tomorrow morning. Then
you can go anywhere you wish!"

We stared at each other. I don't know what I expected,
but it certainly wasn't an announcement of freedom.
Our senses were so numb we had difficulty
comprehending what the young man had said. It wasn't
true, we reasoned. It couldn't be. The Germans were still
lurking in the shadows, or out in the yard, or beyond the
fence in the trees. They would come charging in, their
whips lashing out at us or their rifles blazing. We were
not going to get away so easily.

And even if the Germans weren't there, it seemed
incomprehensible that the Americans would free
us—and so quickly. Ever since we had arrived at the
death camp we had been told what beasts the
Americans were and the terrible things that would
happen if they took the camp. We had not believed the
Nazis, yet something of what they said stuck in our
minds.

"It is true!" the speaker repeated, "Tomorrow you will
be free to leave if you wish.!"

A shout went up. It was feeble at first, and uncertain,

as though we half-expected to be punished for it. Then it picked up in intensity, a swelling volume of sound that threatened to lift the roof and leave the rafters bare of covering.

I shall never forget that day, May 3, 1945. Everyone was shouting and laughing and crying. Tears came from our eyes and rolled, unnoticed, down our cheeks. I, too, was crying as I thanked my God for the deliverance I had long despaired of receiving.

God spared me from knowing at that moment what had happened to my wife and daughter. It was not until much later that I learned of their suffering during the year and a half I was gone.

TEN *"Capitan!"*

IDA

It was a terrible time for mama and I after papa was
taken from the work camp with the rest of the Christian
Jews who were being held there. Except for one
postcard telling us that he was all right, we didn't hear
from him. We didn't know if he was alive, and we didn't
know where he was.

Mama tried to shield me as much as she could, but
she could not keep me from realizing what was
happening to papa. At the age of thirteen I was well
aware of what was going on.

Mama and I lived in her parents' home, a neat

brick-and-stucco structure set well back from the street in a beautiful yard. It was not large by American standards but was one of the nicer homes in our neighborhood: four comfortably sized rooms with a bath. Grandpa had always been very proud of it.

He had anticipated the war and had built a bunker or basement in the yard as a protection against the Russian and American bombing. When we first moved in, mama had only expected to use the bunker for air raids.

But there was an elderly neighbor couple who were also Christians of mixed origins. The wife was a Gentile, the husband a Jew. He had been called in for work at the same time as papa, but he was over sixty years old and not in good health, so they dismissed him.

From the beginning he had been forced to wear the yellow Star of David, but he was one of those who did not have pronounced Jewish characteristics. He had taken advantage of that by hiding his star, wearing it on his coat as he had been ordered but covering it by carrying a book or a parcel. Few people knew of his Jewish origin.

As the bombing increased, these neighbors started coming to our house when the sirens sounded, joining us in the bunker since they had none of their own. When the net went out to gather all those Jews still left in Hungary to ship them off to camps in Austria and Germany, even I knew that might mean death for our dear friend. His body was frail, and he would not be able to withstand the privation he would be subjected to. Mama thought about it and finally decided to invite them to stay in our bunker until it was safe for them to return home. Not long after that she began to hide others, first a woman from Yugoslavia, who was married to a Jew, and her daughter. When they left, two Jewish girls who were friends of the daughter came to stay in the bomb shelter. I'm sure mama knew the risk she was taking. To harbor a Jew was a crime against the state. But she took the chance because of papa.

By June of 1944, the war began to turn against the Germans; every newscast on the "Voice of America" told of new defeats for the Fatherland. We were not supposed to listen to such broadcasts. It was a crime against the state; but we did anyway, turning the volume down so we would not be discovered. It was encouraging to know that the Germans were being defeated, and we gloated inwardly at each new Nazi setback. Their defeat, we reasoned, would bring papa home to us.

Hungarian stations were blaring the news that Russian troops were moving toward our country. The Communist soldiers were portrayed as illiterate beasts completely out of control. We would huddle in the half-basement of my grandparents' house and discuss the broadcasts.

"It isn't true," the Jewish man we were hiding said. "That is only more of the German lies. They want us to be afraid of the Russians and fight against them."

Mother nodded. Although she was of German blood, she would believe nothing the Nazis said.

By Christmas of 1944 the Russians were beginning to squeeze Budapest with giant pincers, their infantry supported by air cover and tanks and heavy artillery. The Hungarian radio stations warned that the Russians were going to force everyone from the suburbs into the heart of the city where they would be

systematically annihilated. By this time it was apparent
to all except the most fervent Nazis that the Allies were
going to win the war.

"*Igen*," mama said confidently. I didn't know if she
really believed what she was saying, or if she was trying
to make life a bit easier for me. "When they take the
camp where he is, they will let him come home."

I thought about that for a moment. It sounded
wonderful, but I still had doubts. "Even if he is a Jew? I
asked. To me, to be a Jew meant persecution.

She eyed me narrowly, wanting to talk more about
that but unsure of what to say. "Even if he is a Jew, Ida."

I find it difficult now to remember just how I felt. I was
young and didn't realize all the bad things that could
happen. Sometimes I would get discouraged and think
that papa had been away for so long we would never see
him again, but mostly I was optimistic and full of hope.
Thinking back, I wonder if God in his mercy didn't
shield those who were young from the full danger we
faced. We laughed and looked forward to one day at a
time.

Only occasionally did fear take hold of me. At first I did
not understand that cold, sickening feeling in the pit of
my stomach—the dread that stole upon me, even when I
felt the most joy. But it was there, unexplainably
coming at the most unlikely of times.

As Christmas came and went, the fighting moved
relentlessly closer to Budapest, until we could hear the
rhythmic explosions of the big guns and the muffled
thunder of heavy equipment being moved into position.
Our suburb was on a fairly large hill, which made the
area of considerable military significance. Control of

our town would provide the Russians with a vantage point on which to locate their tanks and artillery.

The collapse of the German defenders was sudden and, to us, somewhat unexpected, in spite of the encouraging news on the free radio. One moment the arrogant, swaggering Nazis were everywhere. The next, they were not to be seen. Then on the morning of December 31, 1944, we heard the rumble of Russian tanks on our narrow streets and the thunder of big guns pounding the center of Budapest. For the first time I saw panic in my mother's eyes. She did not put her concern into words, but I learned later that she feared the lawless actions of most armies when they take over a new area.

She knew there was no one to help her protect me. Most of the people she knew well were Hitlerites, so she could not expect much assistance from them. When she learned that the Russian army was actually in our village, she grasped my hand and started for the bedroom. "Come, Ida," she said, "quickly."

I looked up, questions gleaming in my eyes. "Where is that kerchief grandma left when they fled to Germany?"

I remember looking around the familiar room, wishing for things to be like they were before the war when mama was not afraid and I could understand what was going on. Nevertheless, I took the scarf from the hook on the back of the door and held it out to her.

"Put it on," she ordered crisply, "and be sure that your hair stays under it."

I wanted to know why, but all she would tell me was that it was very important that I look like an old lady when the Russian soldiers came to our place.

First the tanks moved in on either side of the house we lived in and started firing. The jarring blasts shattered windows and cracked the plaster in the ceiling. We went down to the inside basement with a young man who had stopped to visit us, Tibor Vago, whom I later married, and a friend of his.

I had the impression that mama was disturbed by the damage the concussion was doing to the house, but looking back I don't believe she once considered that. Her mind was fixed on the soldiers who would soon be coming to our door. I saw her lips moving silently and realized that she was praying. Her apprehension kindled the same concern within me, but I could not have explained why. Again I felt that icy emptiness.

Shortly after supper, our first Russian visitors came. Two tall, ruddy, noncommissioned officers greeted mama politely when she opened the door and asked if they could come in. She could speak a little Serbo-Croatian, which is different than Russian, but close enough she could make them understand her. She hesitated momentarily as she would have kept them out if she could have. But they would only have forced their way in, so she stepped aside.

"We are not going to hurt you," the spokesman said as they stomped the snow from their boots. His eyes took in the entire room with one quick, sweeping glance. Watching him, I had the impression he was looking greedily, wondering what he could take for himself.

"You do not have to be afraid," he continued. "We have come to liberate you from our common enemy."

Mama nodded, her expression unchanging.

I could feel their eyes burning into mine. For the first time in my life, a man's look made me shudder. It was an emotion I could not fully understand.

Tibor, who was seventeen at the time, had an eye for me too. I was quite aware that he thought of me as someone very special, and I enjoyed the warmth of his look. There was a purity in it.

"Are there any German soldiers in the house?" the first officer demanded, switching to broken German.

Mama shook her head.

"You—"—he pointed at me—"go upstairs with us and show us there are no German soldiers hiding there."

I glanced quickly at mama, terror in my heart.

"I'll go!" she put in quickly.

"I was talking to her!"

"I go along!" mama repeated firmly. And she went. I looked at her gratefully as we made our way up the steep stairs with the soldiers behind us.

We were ordered to enter each room while they stood just inside the door, their rifles ready. They forced us to open every closet and to get down on our knees with one of them to look under every bed. Only then would they believe that there were no Germans in the house. They relaxed slightly and managed to smile at me.

"It is now New Year's Eve," one of them said. "Can you play?" He gestured at the piano in the room where we were standing.

I nodded mutely.

"All right," he retorted impatiently, "play! This is a time for celebrating."

I sat down at the piano and ran my fingers over the keys. I probably should have been frightened then, but mama had shielded me so well from her own concern that I soon lost my apprehension.

The officers stood a few feet from the instrument, keeping time to the music with their hands. While I was playing, the one who had said nothing since they entered the house moved up behind me quickly and snatched the *babushka* from my head.

Mama sucked in her breath and took a quick, almost involuntary step forward, as though to attack him, but the soldiers did not seem to notice her reaction.

"Old lady!" he exclaimed, contempt edging his voice. "Hmph!"

I realized, then, that he had known all along that I was a young girl and wanted to let us know he had seen through our crude attempt to disguise my age. I was trembling so violently I didn't think I would be able to play any more, but that didn't seem to matter. They had lost interest in the music and ordered us out of the room.

We had just entered the living room when there was a shot outside. One of the men spoke quickly to the other in Russian, and they both bolted through the door, leaving us alone.

ESTER

When those two young officers were in our house, I saw how they stared at Ida. Lust burned within them. It was not their Russian heritage that caused them to be so rapacious and uncontrollable. Such things happened wherever armies went, and Hungary had suffered such treatment at the hands of all her neighbors at one time or another since the days of Rome. We didn't know it then, but such things happened even in the wake of the American troops. To be sure, they usually won their way with candies or food or sheer stockings or the promise of taking a girl to America, while others used force, but the results were the same. The soldiers of whatever army, conducted themselves as they did because they were men, consumed by passion and sin.

Dear God, I prayed in desperation, *protect her. Keep those evil men away from her! Keep her pure and safe and–.* I prayed for myself as well, and for the other women in the house.

As soon as the Russian soldiers dashed out of the house, I took Ida and Tibor down again to the inside basement where the Jewish couple and the two Jewish girls were still hiding. I was glad to have Tibor with us. He was a good Christian boy who went to the same church we did. He would have given his life to keep Ida from being hurt.

We had not been in the basement long when a captain and his aide came to the house and announced that he was going to take over one of the rooms upstairs. Ida could not understand that. "Do we *have* to let them stay?" she demanded impulsively. "It's our house! Can't we make them leave?"

That, of course, was not possible. There was no way we could induce him to take quarters in some other home. But I was thankful for his presence. An officer with the rank of captain, I thought, should have the power to prevent the men in his command from committing rape—and especially in the house where he was living.

I don't remember exactly how many were in our basement that night, but there were quite a few of us. In the grim, uncertain days of war we all helped each other as much as we could. It was not uncommon for us to have a number of neighbors rush to the dubious safety of our basement.

We were crouched there fearfully when a haughty, overbearing, young soldier nineteen or twenty years old swaggered in and surveyed us contemptuously. "You women all to come to the kitchen immediately," he said, "to peel potatoes."

I started to get to my feet and so did Ida, but the wife of the Christian Jew we were harboring laid a restraining hand on my arm. "Don't go," she said urgently. "Don't go!"

"You're to come to the kitchen and peel potatoes," the soldier repeated grimly.

"Don't do it!" my friend warned.

I did not grasp the real purpose of the request immediately, but she was so insistent I did as she said. With my eyes I told Ida to do the same. Two of the women who lived on our block and were in our home did as he requested.

"Mrs. Berger," one of them said softly before going up the steps, "you should come, too. We shouldn't be alone with these soldiers."

However, I remained behind to protect my daughter.

Later we learned that the Russian soldiers took the women into one of the houses nearby and raped them.

After a while another lust-driven soldier arrived.

"Come with me!" he said, pointing to Ida.

Finger of ice gripped my heart and I shook my head in warning.

"Come with me!" he repeated.

"What do you want from a thirteen-year-old girl?" I demanded angrily.

"I don't want you! I want the girl!" he exclaimed. By this time he was losing his temper.

"Go upstairs!" I screamed. "There is a *captain* upstairs!" I cried in Serbo-Croatian. "*Capitan!*" I yelled as loudly as I could. I don't know what I intended to do, but I was not going to allow him to take Ida as long as I was alive. "*Capitan!*" I screamed once more.

At that instant I saw the lust in the drunken young soldier's eyes dim and his gaze wavered uncertainly. He knew that to take a woman by force was forbidden, and he was suddenly afraid that an officer would appear, demanding to know the cause of the commotion. He cursed savagely, and kicked me in the stomach. For one brief, terror-stricken instant I was sure he would squeeze the trigger on his weapon and kill both Ida and me, for she was cowering directly behind me. In that awful moment I was thankful that Ida would be killed if I was. At least she would be spared the terror so many women experienced that night. Instead, the young officer turned and left, slamming the door behind him.

ELEVEN The Root Cellar

TIBOR VAGO

Somehow I had not been taken to Germany by the army, which was strange in itself. Most of the young men my age had long since been drafted. I think God, in his mercy, made it possible for me to be there to help Mrs. Berger and her daughter.

I was not even supposed to be home at the time. I had been sent to western Hungary to work a few months before and had come back to the city for a few days at Christmas. When the holidays were over, the entire city had been surrounded. There was no way I could get back to where I had been working.

Of all the people in our church, I had always admired Mr. Berger more than anyone else. He was not a tall man physically, but he was a giant in his walk with the Lord. Another man was preaching when I took my stand as a believer, along with nineteen other young people, but it was Mr. Berger who had touched a match to my spirit. When he was taken away from his wife and daughter, it was of much concern in our congregation. In our home, as in all others, we prayed every day for them.

The day the Russians stormed our little town, a friend and I went out to see how far away the Russian army was. It was a stupid thing to do, but we thought little of our own safety until soldiers started shooting over our heads. They may have been aiming at us and missed, but I don't believe they were. It seems incredible that they would not have been able to hit us, had they wanted to. They must have been warning us away.

Whatever the reason, we quickly got out of there. Sometimes God takes care of even the very foolish, for the entire area had been heavily mined by the Germans as they retreated. With one false step we could have been blown to pieces.

The next afternoon my friend and I went over to see Mrs. Berger and Ida. Even then, though she was only thirteen and I was four years older, I found her very attractive and sweet.

I was in the basement with them when the fighting surged up and down the streets and among the houses. Because of the battle, it was impossible for anyone to leave safely.

After the young soldier tried to take Ida, her mother and the other women dressed her in the clothes of a very old woman, tied a tattered babushka about her head, and hid her under the wood in a coal box they had in the basement.

We tried to make ourselves believe that the soldiers were not coming back any more that night, but we soon learned otherwise. They were roaming the town like so many wild beasts, stealing everything in sight and ravishing all the women they could find. The same soldier came back to the Berger house a second time, looking for Ida.

"We know she's here!" he exploded, brandishing his weapon at us. "If you don't give her to us, we'll kill you all."

Ida's mother started to argue with him, but he shouted for her to stop. "And this time it will do you no good to shout for the *capitan*. He's not here!".

It was a terrible moment and could have ended in the deaths of everyone in the basement, but one of the Jewish girls the Bergers had been hiding resolved it.

"I'll go with him," she said bitterly. "The Germans took me before. It won't matter if it happens again!"

We didn't want her to go, but she went anyway. They also took the second Jewish girl, who was only a year older than Ida. She was so terrified and was crying so much the Russian soldiers seemed to feel sorry for her. They assured her that she didn't have to be afraid. Finally she accepted the fact that they meant her no harm and stopped crying. She even managed a little smile. We did not see her again, so we don't know what happened to her. The soldiers may have taken her with them, or they may have raped her so many times they killed her. The older girl contracted a disease, but was cured and after the war married a fine man.

There were at least eight soldiers in the house, and I was alone except for the women and the elderly Jewish man. By this time my friend had risked an occasional sniper's bullet to dash for home. Still that night I went upstairs to see if I could help the girls.

I flung the door open, catching a glimpse of the poor girl lying face up on the couch. One soldier was holding her head, and another was already kneeling on her. I leaped forward to jerk him away, but one of the others was ready for me. He swung his rifle by the barrel, hitting me in the head with the heavy wooden stock. My senses reeled and I staggered, almost dropping to my knees. I could not understand what the soldier was shouting at me, but even in my stunned condition I knew I had to get out of there. Somehow I managed to crawl back into the cellar and closed the door.

ESTER

That was one of the worst nights I have ever spent. I had seen brutality before, but never like that. Those soldiers were crazed with liquor and lust—and they would be back. They knew there were women hiding in our house. They would keep returning until none of us would be able to escape them. We were thankful that Tibor was with us, but there was nothing he could do against so many. Still just having him there was a comfort.

As the frigid night wore on we slept a little, but the slightest sound awakened all of us. We would jerk

upright and listen intently for the heavy clump of army
boots or the rich flow of Russian from drunken lips.
Daylight was tracing its gray fingers over the somber
stricken village when there were footsteps and a furtive
knock on the basement door.

"Mrs. Berger," a familiar voice whispered tautly. "Mrs.
Berger, are you there?"

It was Tibor's papa. Wearily I opened the door, and he
stared in at us as though he could scarcely believe what
he was seeing. "Is Tibor here?"

The boy came over to him, explaining that he could
not get home. After Tibor had related our experience, he
asked what had happened at his father's place.

"Nothing." he said. "We had a young soldier staying
with us. He called my wife 'mama' and played chess with
me. He was very nice."

I had supposed that all Russian soldiers were like
those who had made our house a living hell. Now I
had to get used to the fact that there were those who
obeyed their officers and were considerate and
dependable.

Tibor's papa visited with us for a few more moments
and then went back home. No one else came during the
day, but by late afternoon I got to thinking about what
might happen that night. "Quick, Tibor. Run over and
ask your papa if we can stay at his place. We have no
man here, except our Jewish friend."

The boy did as I asked him, and moments later he
came back to tell us it was all right. I knew that it would
be; the Vagos were our friends, as well as our brothers
and sisters in the Lord. The Jewish couple remained at
our house. Because they were elderly, we felt the soldiers

would not hurt them.

We left everything in the house, knowing our
furniture and clothes would be destroyed or stolen
before we returned, and were almost at the Vago house
when a group of soldiers stopped us. They, too, were not
deceived by Ida's disguise. One of them grabbed her
roughly by the shoulders. "She comes with us!"

"TB!" I cried in terror. "She has TB!" I didn't know
that the Russians feared tuberculosis more than any
other disease; the words were an instant reflex to
my terror.

The soldier shrank back fearfully, as though the brief
contact with her would give him the terrible illness. Ida
was safe.

The soldiers also eyed Tibor closely, which made us
realize Ida was not the only one in immediate danger.
The Russians were eager to get strong young men to
help with the hard labor, or even with the fighting.
When we arrived at Vago's house, it was decided that six
of us needed to be hidden—Ida and me, a neighbor
woman, Tibor, and his two sisters.

IDA

Mr. Vago took us into a small shed behind the
building that housed his workshop. Inside was a great
wooden box about three meters square and half a meter
high, with an opening at one end. I don't know what it
had been built for originally, but Tibor's papa was a
farmer and he was always collecting things he might
use in his work. I suppose he thought a box like this

would be a good place to store some of his tools.

"You hide in there," he told us, pointing to the box.

"But they will find us!" I protested. I was much more terrified than I had ever been before.

"No one even knows this shed is here," he replied. "And if they should find it and come inside, we will have the box well covered with roots. They will not find you here, Ida. That I guarantee."

His words of assurance were not enough to quiet my fears, but everyone else was in agreement with him. I had to do as they said.

All six of us got into the box quietly. I constantly felt that I was suffocating, but that was not the worst part. When we were all inside, it was only possible for us to move a few inches either way. There was not even room for us to lay on our sides. It wasn't long until every muscle we possessed throbbed with pain.

I lay in the box fighting for breath and listening intently for any sound that would indicate the soldiers were on the prowl. The old shed groaned and creaked in the wind, and with every change of sound, I thought there was a soldier coming after me. I had always had a very vivid imagination and had been able to tie myself in knots with worry. Now the very real danger we were experiencing was multiplied a thousand times by the fantasies I called to mind.

At first I had not noticed the heat in the tight box. It was winter time and there was no fire in the shed. Yet, it was not long until the heat from our bodies made our hiding place stifling. I tried to sit up, but bumped my head. I lay back, trembling.

The Russians were in the house by this time, I told

myself. They had come and beaten Tibor's papa and mama until they had told where we were hiding. In a moment or two they would bring those evil men to the shed to get us. I wondered whether they would kill me or take me the way they had taken the two Jewish girls.

Why couldn't those men be like Tibor? He was kind and gentle, and would not let anything happen to me, I told myself. But then I remembered that he had not been able to help the Jewish girls.

I finally drifted off to sleep, praying for God's protection. As I lost consciousness I remember thinking that I could not possibly stand being cooped in the box until morning. I didn't see how I could do it for an hour, but somehow God gave us extra grace and patience. We were able to survive until daylight when Mr. Vago came to the shed, moved the roots, and helped us out of the big box. We stayed in the house until just before dark; then he moved us to a hole he had dug in the yard for storing potatoes, carrots and other root vegetables. It was three-or-four meters deep and two-or-three meters square, a crudely dug hole, designed to protect the vegetables from freezing. The entrance was narrow and steep, slanting down to the floor of the cellar.

By this time the nice, well-mannered soldier Tibor's papa had told us about had moved on. The next one heard that there were women on the place, and he was determined to find them. Mr. Vago could understand him fairly well, but he pretended not to.

"They're here!" the Rusian blurted angrily. "People have seen them during the day. They've got to be here at night, too."

Mr. Vago shrugged his shoulders expressively,

indicating by his actions that he did not know what the other man was saying.

"There is no point in lying to me!" the soldier repeated angrily.

They were standing in the yard, and the Russian was almost in the entrance way, so close to where we were hiding that we could hear almost everything he said. All he had to do was look around, and he would see the opening.

"You'd better tell me where they are," he threatened. In his desperation he tried to speak in Hungarian, but he was completely unintelligible. Then he tried sign language. Again Tibor's papa informed him by motions that only they lived in the house. That was true. We were hiding in a hole in the yard.

The next morning, as soon as it was light, Mr. Vago set to work, changing the entrance to our hiding place. He filled in the excavation that led into the root cellar, leaving only a small opening at ground level—one that he could easily cover with a few pieces of wood and hide with dirt and corn husks. Next he built a rough ladder for us to use in coming out of the hole and going down again. We only had a bucket for a toilet. Three times a day one of those still in the house would watch closely while someone else would take food to us and exchange buckets, an empty one for the full.

Others came to the shelter from time to time. By the end of a month of hiding, sixteen people had sought safety in the root cellar.

We had a small kerosene lamp in the hole and our Bibles, which we all read a great deal. And we sang, softly. One song was my favorite. I had never heard it before, nor have I heard it since, although I have been told it is also in English: "How Tedious Are the Hours without Jesus." We clung to the words of that song like a drowning man to a rope.

The Vagos did not have enough food for so many, but there was food at our home. During the day, Mr. Vago would take a wheelbarrow and go over and get something for us to eat. He didn't tell us what was happening to our house and we did not ask. I am sure that neither mama nor I gave any thought to the house or our furniture, or even our clothes.

The days wore on, and the soldiers were slowly brought under control by their officers. When the Vagos felt it was safe, they suggested that we come out of the hole for a little while during the day.

On one occasion, a soldier came to the house unexpectedly while we were there. He didn't say anything, but we could feel his eyes burning into us and we squirmed uncomfortably. As soon as it was dark he came back, looking for us.

"Where are the women?" he demanded.

"What women?"

"Those women who were here this afternoon."

"There are only the two of us," Tibor's papa said, indicating his wife.

The man's eyes darkened with rage. "You know where they are! Tell me or I'll kill you!"

"Look for yourself. There are no women here!"

He clumped through the house in his futile search, Tibor's papa at his side. Then he stormed out into the moon-drenched yard, his piercing eyes searching for some hiding place large enough to keep us out of sight.

Fortunately it had snowed late in the afternoon—not much, but enough to cover our tracks and to help the corn husks and cobs camouflage the opening into our man-made cave.

"I will give you one last chance. Tell me where they are or it will go hard with you."

Down in the bunker I was trembling. Surely Mr. Vago would break now and tell where we were hiding. I could almost feel the soldier's rough hands on my shoulders. But Tibor's papa did not weaken. It was as though he had no fear.

TWELVE   A New Order

ESTER

I will never forget the morning Ida and I left our hiding
place in the Vagos's yard and went back to see how our
house had fared during our absence. It had snowed
several times while we were away, but a week or so
before, the weather had warmed, melting much of the
snow cover. As it always did at that time of year, it
turned cold once more, and we had to pick our way over
the remaining drifts and frozen ground to reach my
father's home.

From around the corner we could see that a part of
our roof was gone, torn off by a shell aimed at the tanks

that had been parked on either side of the house. A sudden nausea twisted my stomach into a hard, icy knot, and I felt the strength go out of my legs.

"Look, Ida!" I exclaimed, forgetting for the moment that I had to remain strong to bolster her spirits.

As we drew closer, we could see that the concussion of the big guns had knocked out most of our windows. But that was nothing compared to the destruction that had been done to the interior. Everything left in the house had been ripped apart or stolen by vandals. Pictures had been pulled from the walls and thrown carelessly onto the big pile of furniture, linen, and clothes in the living room. Chair rungs and seats were broken and my beautiful linen scarves and tablecloths had been torn into rags and used as towels. The entire mess was locked together by a thick slab of ice from the melting snow that had piled high in the upstairs rooms, most of which were roofless. My fingers tightened impulsively over Ida's trembling hand.

Mechanically we went from one room to the other, surveying the damage. There were a few pieces of furniture left. "Our piano was right in here," Ida said softly. "Where is it now, mama?"

I shook my head, a great weariness stealing over me.

Her eyes flashed. "Someone must have stolen it!"

I did not reply. We found it later in a neighbor's house and brought it back. There were those who took advantage of the turmoil and absence of law to do as they pleased.

"Can we fix the house?" Ida demanded. "Will we *ever* be able to live in it again?"

"*Igen*," I said sternly. "We will fix it!" I didn't know

just how, but we would!

Tibor came over and worked on our house. Before he started, I didn't see how we could ever live in it again. Much of the roof was torn away, and there was broken glass everywhere. First he rebuilt the roof so the rain and snow could not come in. Then he set to work on the windows. We had no glass to replace that which had been broken out, so he used wood, nailing boards over each opening. It made the house dark, but it did hold out the weather, which was most important. Once our house was livable, we moved back.

The first thing Ida did was walk from room to room, her young face reflecting her dismay. "It isn't nice like it was before," she said. "Do you think we will ever have it back the way it was?"

I hesitated. I felt that same emptiness, that same feeling of sadness and frustration. "*Igen*," I told her. "When papa comes home, he will fix it."

She turned her big eyes on me, and I saw fear lurking in those deep, luminous recesses. I didn't know what she was thinking, and I didn't ask. But it hurt to see the dread that lurked there. One so young should be happy and lighthearted. But how could we expect the children to be happy when there was so much misery all about them?

As for me, I still had hope that all would be well again. Sandor would come back, I told myself. But I had no assurance. Over and over again I would ask myself, Why? Why would God take Sandor? He was not like other men. He always thought of God first, then Ida, then me, and finally of himself. In the homes of our neighbors, if the wife had bread or a small cake left over in the baking, it was always saved for the father. If I had something left over—even something Sandor especially liked—he would tell me to give it to Ida.

Why should such a one be taken when others who were selfish and uncaring were left behind? Often I asked God about such things, but there was no answer.

Still, there was no rebellion in my heart. Sandor would not have liked it. I could almost hear his mild voice: "If God wants me here, he has a purpose in it. If he wants me at home, he will take care of me and see that I get there." His tone would speak even louder than his words, cautioning me, "Be patient, Ester, be patient." I tried, but it was so very hard!

I had known one neighbor and her family since my parents moved to the neighborhood. After my parents went to Germany, this family moved into the little house on the back of my parents' lot, but we didn't think anything about that. It was wartime, and we were all caught in a terrible conflict.

During the battles that freed Budapest from Nazi hands, the little house was bombed so it was not livable, and they rented an apartment nearby. Still, they considered the small house theirs.

You have to understand the family to know why I felt as I did toward them. That woman and her children were never strong for work. They always wanted something for nothing. She came back to the yard and picked the cherries and tore the wooden fence down for fuel. Even though the property belonged to my family, I was hardly able to benefit from it.

One day when I found her in the yard, I lost my temper. "There is not enough for you to take everything you want!" I exploded. "We need something, too. And it is ours—not yours!"

She was angry, and decided that she would do something to get back at me. But that was not all. She had her eye on my parents' property, the house Ida and I were living in. She wanted it for herself.

It wasn't long until she went down to the authorities and notified them that my parents had gone to Germany, and that the property we lived in was theirs. I had my own smaller place, she told them, but I did not live in it. I had moved into my parents' home. The two of us lived in five rooms, while she had to live with her large family in a two-room apartment.

Three men from the government came out to see me, representatives of each party. There was a Socialist, a Communist, and a Democrat. It was frightening for both Ida and me. They looked so official, so stern as they wrote down a list of all we had.

"It is a bad thing that you have so much and the people who used to live in the small house on your parents' property have so little," they said to me. "You should go back to your own house. We want this one."

I argued that they could not take the property away, but I knew that if they decided to do as they said, there was nothing I could do to stop them.

"The law will decide if you can stay in this house," one of the men said.

My neighbor saw me in the yard after the men were gone, her eyes bright with triumph. "One of these days you will go back to your house. I will go into the one you live in now."

I talked with Ida about it that evening. I had always

been sure the woman was after our house, but I never had any proof. Now she had told me herself. To lose the house would be hard enough, to lose it to her—that I could not stand.

It was a long legal battle. When the day of the decision came, I went down to the Town House and stood in line. I had been there an hour when an officer came out to question me. When he learned that there were only two of us in a house that was large enough for more, he said they would have to take the house from us.

"If there were more people living there, we would let you stay," he said.

If only I had known, I might have been able to do something about it. There were many we knew who needed places to stay. Now it was too late. They were going to take it away from us in a few minutes. I was so upset I wasn't even thinking that God could intercede for me. I did not even pray to him as I stood in the line. To me, our case was hopeless.

My turn before the officer in charge was drawing close, when a Jewish man, his son, and his son's girl friend entered the building. They were complaining bitterly that they had no place to live. "Everybody is asking questions of us," the older one said, "but nobody asks, 'Have you food or have you somewhere to live?'"

I called them over. "I will give you a room and furniture," I said. "You can live with us."

It was agreed in an instant. Together we appeared before the officer in charge. Before the officer spoke, the Jewish man told him that I was going to give a room to the three in his family. The officer agreed and started to type up the papers. He was halfway through the form when he stopped and said, "What is the name of your property?"

"Schmidt," I told him.

His gaze slowly left the paper and came up to meet mine. His cheeks tinged with crimson, and for an instant his lips quivered. He suddenly realized that this was the property they were planning to give to my neighbor. But he had already told the Jewish man that his family could live with us, and that I could keep the house if they moved in.

If our roomers had not been Jews, we learned later, the authorities would have told them to go, and they would have taken the house from us anyway. But they were trying to make it look as though they were good to Jews, in contrast to the Germans. God had intervened at just the right time and in exactly the right way to make it possible for us to keep the house.

THIRTEEN Freedom!

SANDOR

After the Americans came and we realized we were
actually free, we did a very foolish thing. We broke into
the German stores of food and ate everything we could
find: cheeses and breads, canned meat and fruit.

We had not finished stuffing ourselves when the
Americans came with eggs—cases and cases of eggs,
piled in the back of a large vehicle. We were given all we
wanted without having to pay. We had no fires to cook
them, but that made no difference. We were so hungry
for eggs, we cracked the shells and poured the delicious
substance down our throats.

We ate and ate and ate until our stomachs rebelled, and we lost by vomiting much of what we had stuffed down our throats. Yet we wanted more. Today I cannot understand such wanton gorging. It does not seem reasonable that adult men would eat until they were sick and still go back another time. It was as if we were afraid all the food would disappear, and we would again be starving.

Some died from overeating that day.

The Americans told us we could stay in the camp for a little while, or we could leave. No longer would guards be over us, prodding us out of bed in the morning, forcing us to stand at attention for two or three hours at a time, shooting us at random every evening. But few of us wanted to remain in the camp any longer. We had homes in Hungary and were as anxious to get back to them as soon as possible.

Most of us left the next day. There were no trains out of the village in the direction we wanted to go, so a large group of us began trudging slowly toward Budapest.

My brother and I walked together in comparative silence. Actually, there was little talking and no laughing or excitement. Everyone was so drained of strength and emotion that we had little more life than when we had marched the other direction under the cruel prodding of the Nazis. Looking at us, one might have assumed that an invisible army was still oppressing us, daring us to smile or laugh or talk loudly.

I had the feeling that this was not actually happening to me. I was on some high hill looking down on the ragged line of former prisoners moving in dejection toward home. Or I was still a captive dreaming of freedom, but knowing that I would soon awaken to the hunger and tyranny of another day.

Too much had happened to us in the last seventeen months for us to shrug off our misery. We had to learn to think and laugh again, to go where we wished and do as we pleased.

I had completely forgotten the large detachment of Jewish workers we had seen when we were being taken to the death camp, until we approached the city of Wells. I supposed that they had been released and were back with their families again. I was so sure of that, I was surprised to hear myself asking a farmer about them.

"Them?" the bent, gray-haired farmer echoed, a strange tone in his voice. "When the Nazis decided to pull out, they shot and killed the whole lot.

I stared incredulously at him. That could not be true, I told myself.

Reading the doubt in my face, he added, "It's the truth. I saw the bodies myself, after it was over."

How jealous I had been of those Jews because they were getting enough to eat and were being fairly well treated. I had complained bitterly to God because I and those with me were being singled out for torture when that group of Jews had much to make them comfortable. Now those I had envied were dead, and I was alive.

Tears streamed down my gaunt cheeks as I asked God to forgive me. I had learned again the truth of the Bible verse, "All things work together for good to them that love the Lord." God had shown his marvelous loving-kindness and care to me, something I did not deserve.

We were in Wells when word came that the Nazi government had surrendered. The Austrian people, who had been forced to fight on the side of their powerful neighbors, were delirious with joy. They ran through the streets shouting, "The war is ended!" And when they saw us, tears flowed from their eyes. They had been forced to stand helplessly by while we were being abused and killed.

By the time we reached Wells most of us were ill. I suppose we had been sick when we left the death camp but were too overwhelmed by all that had happened to realize it. Once we arrived at this city, we knew we were sick and went to the hospital, where more of our number died.

We had scrub typhus, a disease carried by rodents and tainted food in the Mediterranean area. I am sure that malnutrition and our stuffing ourselves after our release had something to do with the savage way the disease hit us. For days I lay close to death, burning with fever. I was delirious at times, drifting in and out of consciousness, little caring what happened to me. I didn't even protest when they took my Bible from me, because they feared it might contaminate others in the hospital and cause them to come down with the same ailment.

My brother, Stephen, was ill, too, but only for a few days. He had not been so long in a concentration camp. Because of his skills, the Germans had kept him working in a factory where he got plenty to eat and a clean place to live. Life had not been easy for him, but he was in better physical condition than most of us.

Stephen had much to do with my recovery. The

Americans helped as much as they could, but they did not have enough of the right foods to take care of everyone. Each day my brother went out and begged food for me, especially milk. The doctor said I had to have a great deal of milk and milk products like cheese.

Stephen didn't go to the people in the city, but to those who lived in the small towns around Wells. They were the ones who had the cows and made cheeses. They were the ones who had food for themselves and could spare a little for me. We were all amazed at the kindness of those men and women who had so little, except food. Who could have found fault with them if they had placed a high price on what they had? But they knew the horrors of war, and they shared with us. As I recovered enough to realize what they were doing, I thanked God daily for them. I don't know what would have happened to me had it not been for their generosity.

It was several weeks until I could think straight once more. A friend of mine from before the war came frequently to the hospital for treatment. He, too, was a Jew and had been held in a camp. He had professed to be a Christian, but his faith was only in his head. Still, he had been a good man and I had seen something fine in him, a gentleness that set him apart from the others.

That was before he was torn from his family and put in a prison camp. When he came to the hospital, the gentleness was gone. He was hard where once he had been kindly. He was blasphemous and profane where his language had once been clean. I had never seen such a change in an individual. His manner was harsh and belligerent. His patience had fled, and he was short-tempered and fought with everyone.

I used to think about him during my stay in the hospital, wondering what had caused him to become so different. He had suffered much, it was true, but no more than many of the others I knew. The only explanation was that he had not had the Lord to give him strength and encouragement. Without Christ, he had become almost like the men who had so ruthlessly tortured us.

Even though we were now free, there was little joy and happiness. Fear still crowded in on us, sneaking in at the corners of our minds, waking us at night with horrible dreams that left us shaken and trembling. Fear caused us to be wary of those in the beds next to us, even though they, too, were Jews who had suffered as we had suffered.

One man wept continually for his wife and children. They had been stuffed into a gas chamber some months before, while he had been spared to help the Nazi war machine. Life had ceased to have purpose and meaning for him. He could think only of the fact that everyone in the world that he loved was gone, yet he had to live.

The man in the bed on the other side of me kept wanting to go home. He, too, had lost his entire family, but that did not cause him to change his determination. He talked about going home to anyone who would listen, and to those of us who were forced to because we had a bed close to his. And he mumbled about it in his dreams at night. It was the only subject on his tortured mind.

We Jews had good reason to be disturbed. Before the war, there were 600,000 of us scattered across

Hungary. When it was over, there were only 17,000 still alive, less than one Jew in thirty-five.

After six weeks, I felt better and was able to be released from the hospital. The Americans put us in a big palace with a great yard where we were to wait until we could get transportation home. We got good food, nice sleeping quarters, and complete freedom to do as we pleased. There I met a neighbor who had not been in the hospital and was able to go home earlier than I. He promised to tell Ester and Ida that I was alive and would be coming home soon.

In this place were Jews who came from countries other than Hungary. And there were also those who had volunteered to serve the Nazis. They had treated the rest of us very badly, and I know they did not like being kept with us, but there was no way for them to get home unless they did. So they changed their clothing, hoping to hide themselves.

I was walking in the yard one afternoon when I heard a cry. A German name was being called out very loudly. We saw that a dozen or fifteen boys from ten to twelve years old had thrown themselves on a tall adult, throwing him to the ground. "You Nazi gangster!" they shouted, beating him with their fists. "Why were you so cruel to us?"

I think they would have killed him if the American soldiers had not shot in the air to silence them. "He is a wicked man," one of them told the boys, "but let him come before the court to be punished."

Reluctantly they allowed the soldiers to take the man away, to be held in jail until he could be tried for his crimes. If those boys had killed that man, it would have haunted them the rest of their lives.

When I was able to travel, I started walking again with another Jewish fellow. At the next town, he stopped at a camp set up to care for Jews until they could get back home. I did not want to wait any longer, so I walked alone for three days to Sopron, the Hungarian city just across the border from Austria.

Sopron was filled with Jews from all over Eastern Europe. Someone has estimated there were at least fifty thousand Jews from that part of the continent trying to get back to their homes. Feeding them and supplying transportation for many was a staggering task. Big kitchens had been set up and the Americans, with the help of Hungarian volunteers, were trying to feed everyone. "There are so many of you," we were told, "that nobody should come twice through the line."

But we were still hungry and recently from a place where we had looked out only for ourselves. I had often prayed that God would help me to think of others before myself. Yet, when I finished eating and saw that everyone else was washing their bowls and going back for more, I did the same. As I came through the line a second time, one of those who was serving recognized me.

"Mister!" he exploded, loudly enough for all to hear, "I did not think you would stoop to coming through again when others have not eaten!"

I cringed under his withering glare. He didn't say so, but I believe he must have known of my Christian testimony. I wanted to ask him, but I was trembling so from guilt that I could only think of slinking out of sight. I started to leave, but his strident voice followed me.

"It is such a disgrace! Are you not ashamed of what you tried to do?"

But it was not his words that stabbed me as I headed for the railway station. It was the look in his eyes and the tears that trickled down his cheeks. He was so deeply concerned for those who needed food that he was as shaken by what had happened as I.

If I had ever thought I was more honorable than the others, I lost it that day. God was showing me that I had to constantly turn to him for guidance, that I had to trust him to help me if I wanted to live as I should. When I tried to decide things for myself, I was little better than those who did not know him.

At the railway station I waited for the train to Budapest, alone in the surging crowd of people. There were at least one thousand Jewish men at the station, waiting for a train that would take them home. I realized that it would be a long, tiring trip.

When I got to Budapest, I stopped at a bakery where I bought some pastry goods with the remaining money the Americans had given me for food. The pastry was nothing like that Ester made, but never had I tasted anything quite so good as it did that morning. I had had no rolls or pie or cake since I had been sent to the school in Budapest over a year and a half ago, and I loved baked goods.

From the bakery, I went to the home of Ester's uncle. I was anxious to get to the suburb where my wife and daughter were waiting for me, but I dreaded it too. I don't know why, except that we had been separated for so long and I was so drained of emotion that I felt dead and wooden inside. It was as though I had lost my capacity to respond or to show any sign of affection. I wanted to see them, I wanted it desperately; yet I wanted to put off the the reunion.

Ester's uncle gave me some food and a hat and a jacket. He was a larger man than I. The hat came down over my ears, giving me a grotesque, clownlike appearance that caused us all to laugh. The jacket was big enough to go around me twice with some left over. The shoulders went a third of the way to my elbows, and the sleeves swallowed my hands when I let my arms hang.

"You don't have to wear them, Sandor," he told me.

"*Igen*," I said quickly, "I will wear them. The hat and coat are big, but they will be nice when it gets colder."

Then I left for the town on the outskirts of Budapest where Ester and Ida were waiting for me.

FOURTEEN The Road Back

ESTER

I will never forget the afternoon Sandor came home from the camps. I was working in the kitchen when the bell sounded. I was annoyed that I had to stop what I was doing, wipe my hands on a towel, and answer the door.

A wizened little man in a coat six sizes too large and with a hat to match was standing there. At first I did not recognize him. Sandor has never been large, but the individual standing before me was hunched and wasted, a mere scarecrow of a man. The thought came that it had to be a child standing in my doorway—a neighbor boy or girl who was playing "dress up." His bony features were only vaguely familiar, and his sunken eyes were dull and expressionless, as though they opened onto a barren soul. I was about to ask whom he wanted—to tell him that there was no one in the house except myself and my daughter—when something about the way he was looking at me caused me to realize who it was. My shoulders trembled and the color fled from my face, leaving it a sickly, ashen gray.

"Sandor!" I said softly. It was surprising that he even heard me, my voice was so weak with emotion.

He answered simply, as though he had been asked the time and was responding. "Yes," he said. "I am Sandor."

I had often dreamed of the time when he could come home, the delirious tears of joy, the loud talking, the laughter. But the actual event was not that way. I put my arms about him and kissed him tenderly, but there was little response on his part. It was almost as though we were strangers. Only when we went inside did the excitement of his returning home explode upon me. I had him sit on the sofa and took my place beside him, my arm about his frail shoulders. I could have cried when I felt the hard corners of his bones beneath the coat. It was as though he was a skeleton with only a thin layer of flesh to cover his slight frame. He sat motionless, completely drained of strength, a frail, lifeless shadow of the man who had been taken from us by the Germans.

"Where have you been, Sandor?" I wanted to know. Now that I had started talking, the words tumbled out, one falling upon another until they were all but unintelligible. "Have you been well? When you were in the camp, were they mean to you? Did they give you enough to eat?"

I knew the answer to my question without being told. I looked down and saw his bloated stomach, a silent indication of starvation and malnutrition.

"Sandor, tell me what it was like in camp."

He pulled in a loud, deep breath, and his gaze met mine. His lips parted and I thought he was going to speak, but he did not until I repeated the question another time.

"Hard," he said grimly. "It was hard."

That was the way he answered my every question, tersely and with no explanation, if he answered at all. I pressed to find out more about the ordeal, and so did Ida when she came home.

I had never seen her so happy, not since her father had been away. Her heart sang, and she all but danced about the room. I noticed that Sandor's eyes followed her hungrily, as though just seeing her again was food and drink to him. I suppose he was looking at me in the same way, but when he saw that I was watching him, he turned away quickly, embarrassed that I caught him looking at me.

Later, when Ida and I again asked what had happened to him, he was even less communicative than he had been when I first tried to find out. It was as though he now had the capacity to draw within himself and lock everyone else on the outside.

Ida could not understand the change that had come over him in the months he had been away—his lack of responsiveness and the absence of any display of love. "What is wrong with papa?" she whispered to me after he had gone to bed. "Doesn't he care about us any more?"

"He cares," I told her firmly. "Of course he cares. It is just hard for him now. He has been treated so badly, it hurts even to think about those things."

In the months that followed, I had the same feelings about Sandor myself. I thought there must have been something I had done or hadn't done to make him unhappy. "If I have hurt you," I told him many times, "I am sorry. I haven't meant to."

Those sunken eyes would fix on me, staring from some deep, dark abyss that I could not understand. "No, Ester, it is not that," he would say and his voice would fade. "It is nothing you have done. It's—" He would get slowly to his feet and pace to the nearest window where he looked for a long while out at the narrow street.

I don't think either Ida or I understood how ill he had been, or what terrible effect his long imprisonment had on him.

SANDOR

Few of the Jewish survivors were spared physical and mental problems, and I was no different than the others. For months after I got back, I would black out and fall down periodically from the weakness following my bout with typhus and a serious lack of vitamins.

For two or three years I had frequent nightmares that took me back to those terrible camps. I would waken in the middle of the night, wrapped in sweat, every fiber of my body trembling. I relived, again and again, the beatings, the dehumanizing punishments, the fear that was constantly with us. When those dreams came, sleep was finished for the night, and the next day or two I was haunted by the scenes my subconscious had called to the surface.

Ester had only been able to save a few of my clothes, and I had brought back with me only those I was wearing. I would have had no coat or hat if her uncle had not shared with me, and my shoes were completely gone. The stores had nothing in them back in those days. Few had even reopened, so we could not have bought anything if we had had the money.

Ester rummaged through the house and came up with an old pair of her brother's ski boots. He was taller than I by a third of a meter, and his feet were correspondingly larger, which didn't make for a good fit, but I was thankful for anything to wear.

I knew Ida and Ester wanted to laugh when they first saw me in them, but they were too kind for that. However, a sixteen-year-old girl in church saw me and almost became hysterical.

"Oh, Uncle Berger!" she gasped. "Big feet!"

I didn't mind. I knew how those boots must look on me. I normally wore a size 7 and those were 11's, and ski boots.

I had to wear my ski boots and my big coat when I began to preach. They were all I had. But the people didn't seem to object. They were pleased to have someone who could bring them God's Word.

At first I could not think straight enough to give a sermor It was as though my mind was dead, and I had not the strength to force it to life. I wanted to preach once more, but I didn't know whether I could do it or not until a delegation for the church came to see me.

"You know our deacon has been preaching to us since you were away," the spokesman began.

"*Igen.*" I knew him well. He was at least seventy-two years old now but had done a fine job of preaching to hold the church together during the war.

"Well, he feels that he no longer has the strength to keep on preaching, and we have no one who is capable of taking his place—except you. Will you help us, Brother Berger?"

Help them? I asked myself. How could I help them? I found it difficult enough to study the Bible. How could I organize my thoughts to share God's Word with them, when I found it hard to talk to Ester and Ida about simple things like the garden or the paint the house needed? In detention fear had driven us to silence. Now that I was free again the habit was not easily broken.

But the delegation was so sure I was the one to minister to them that I could not refuse. I felt God had sent them. To turn them down would have been to go against what he wanted me to do.

As soon as they left I got my Bible and began to read, this time with more purpose than I had had in months. I was glad they had come to me early in the week. At least I had some time to prepare. But it was difficult. I could not even find a subject that gripped me. It was as though I was lifeless, a creature without emotion, almost without the ability to think constructively. I could read the Bible, but any comprehension was gone. The words were like sawdust to a hungry man: flat, tasteless, and empty. I knew it was not the Bible that was different. It was me. I had seen too much—had experienced too much—to react normally to anything.

I closed the Book and strode to the window where I watched the street without seeing. Was I useless to God? Would I ever be able to serve him again?

If I cannot serve you, Father! I cried inside myself. *Please take me home!"*

But those desperate thoughts changed nothing. I had agreed to preach to a group of his people; I must try, even if I failed. I went back to the desk and began to read again. Slowly, as I read his Word, the subject for my first sermon came to me. I cannot remember what it was now, but I know I avoided Scripture that dealt with suffering. The promises that were dear to me were those that offered hope for the future.

Yet, the sermon did not come easily even after I knew what I was to speak about. Every thought—every Scripture reference had to be wrestled with. I still felt so helpless I was sure I could not finish the message. When Sunday came, I knew I was going to be speechless. But I had promised, so I kept on working. That sermon took longer to develop than any message I had ever prepared before. When Sunday came, I had it finished.

I spoke fearfully, and I am sure I did not do very well. But the people were kind, and I knew there were those who were praying for me. The longer I spoke the stronger my voice became, and my self-assurance came seeping back to strengthen me. By the time I finished the message, I knew God had directed my return to the pulpit. That was not the last personal battle I had in preparing a sermon. Every week it was a struggle to find a subject that would be helpful to the people, and I was so slow in preparation that it almost seemed a miracle when I had something ready for Sunday. But each sermon became a little easier to prepare.

The borough council was aware that I had started preaching again, but they said nothing to me at first. That was in the early days of the regime, when they were boasting that they were going to allow complete freedom of religion and were making Hungary a better, happier place for everyone. People were to have no difficulties with their rulers, they said. The entire country was to be free. The large land holdings of the very wealthy were taken away, and smaller plots given to the farmers who lived nearby. We were to come and go as we pleased, with no interference from anyone. Christian and Jew alike were to be able to worship as they pleased, even though the government officially denied the existence of God. Party members even came out to help rebuild the churches, so they could be used again.

Everybody thought it was to be a good government, in spite of the Stalinist influence. But I had only been preaching a little while when I received a summons from one of the party leaders in our village. We had both lived in the community for years and knew each other very well.

What if this were to be the beginning of another long period of imprisonment and torture? I asked myself. The Germans had pushed me to the thin edge of endurance. Now that I had freedom and a time without fear, I didn't think I could withstand another concentration camp. As I made my way to the local office, I talked to God about it, telling him how afraid I was and how much I feared the Stalinist influence on our government. I told him I wanted to stand true to my faith in Jesus Christ, but that I could not do it alone.

When I arrived at the plainly furnished office, the leader came around his desk to shake hands with me. He was warm and kindly, so I began to relax as we talked.

"Mr. Berger," he said at last, his voice gentle and compassionate, "you went through some very hard things during the past two years. Now I think you know where your place is."

He was talking about my place in the party, of course, but I pretended not to be aware of it. "Yes," I said, "I know where my place is. I am in my place."

I don't know what his reaction was, or whether he even caught the meaning of my words, but he smiled and shook hands to indicate that the little visit was over.

Ester was waiting anxiously for me to come home, and was relieved to learn that nothing serious had happened.

"But I'm afraid it isn't over," I reminded her wearily. "It is just beginning."

"Perhaps you are wrong, Sandor," she countered hopefully. "Perhaps they really are different than the Stalinists. I am going to pray for them."

I remained silent, allowing her to grasp for some shred of hope.

A few days later, I was contacted again and asked to come down to the party office to do some work for them. When I got there, I was introduced to a man I assumed to be a newcomer because I had never seen him before.

"You two will be going out together," they told me.

"You are to talk to the people and tell them that there is no God."

Numbly I stared at the officer. Tell the people that there is no God? The words rang in my ears. How could I, of all men, deny the existence of Almighty God? He had not only saved me by his death on the cross, he had kept me alive in both body and spirit during those awful devastating months when the Nazis held me captive. He had cared for Ester and Ida during their times of need, and now he provided food for us when others were suffering greatly, some even starving. I wanted to speak my heart to the party leader, to tell him that I could not do as he asked, regardless of what might happen to me. But I could not bring myself to do it. I was so frightened, I was powerless to speak. So he took my silence for agreement.

At the first home we visited, my companion asked a question. "Would you say there is no God?"

Then he turned to me and indicated that I should continue the conversation. I hesitated momentarily, desperation gripping me. I was frightened, as frightened as I had ever been, except for the period I was in the death camp. My heart hammered against my thin chest, and sweat beaded my forehead. "Nobody can prove that there is no God," I stammered.

My companion seemed surprised but made no effort to contradict me.

At the next house I came out a little stronger, sharing a bit of what had happened to me in the concentration camps, relating how God had strengthened and comforted me. I did the same on our other calls that afternoon, but not without concern. I was sure I was ending my freedom. My companion would report me as soon as we finished that afternoon.

And he must have, for I was never sent out on such an assignment again. However, I do not know why they didn't do something to me. Perhaps they still had hopes of persuading me to embrace their brand of atheism. Or, maybe they didn't want to come down too harshly on those of us who did not agree with them. Tolerating us could give them the appearance of a benevolent, free society.

But I was not forgotten. The borough council let me know as much by inviting me to a party meeting at their hall. Again I didn't want to go, but was afraid not to. At the meeting, the man who had been my companion on visitation got up when his turn came and said flatly, "There is no God."

A muted round of clapping went up in approval, and the leaders on the platform smiled indulgently. This was the sort of talk they wanted to hear. It indicated that they would soon be accomplishing their purpose. After a few moments, the chairman asked if there were any questions.

There was no movement in the big room until I got to my feet. I didn't know what I was going to say, but I could not leave without witnessing for my Christ, even though I had to do it indirectly.

"I am very interested that you say there is no God," I began. "Please tell us more. How did you reach that conclusion? What is the evidence?"

There was a brief pause and the men on the platform glanced uncertainly at each other, color creeping into their cheeks. The chairman acted as though he was about to get to his feet but didn't quite dare. Another party faithful stirred uneasily, as though he felt he should do something but didn't know how. Finally the chairman asked if there were any more questions and adjourned the meeting.

How I thanked God for giving me the courage to speak out, and the wisdom to say what I did. I could not be criticized for that. There was no evidence that I was taking a position counter to the official line on religion. However, I began to understand what they were about. They were going to wait and allow their incessant propaganda against Christ and the church take its effect.

A few days after the meeting, I was in a nearby suburb on business. It was a holy day, and when I went past the Catholic Church very early that morning, I saw the party member who had publicly said there was no God. He was kneeling in prayer.

Poor man! How it must have torn at him to be like Peter and deny our Lord. I could not criticize him. I knew why he had done it. He feared losing his position within the party, or even stronger action.

The authorities continued to try to persuade me to hold their Communist beliefs, but that was useless. I continued to preach and started attending Bible seminary classes at night to better prepare myself.

FIFTEEN   Where God Wants Me

Everything changed after the election in 1948, when the government claimed they had a mandate from the people to put their full progam into effect. For months before the election, they had been calling in the heads of households, and everyone else who was working, to fill out long, detailed questionnaires:

Where do you work?
What do you do?
Where do you live?
Do you have any relatives in the West?
Do you keep in touch with them?
Do you believe in God?
Do you go to church?

From the questionnaires, the government formed
two lists: one contained the names of those whom they
considered loyal and "safe." The other was made up of
those who were suspected of being enemies of the state.
Christians were on the latter. The council let us know
that we could lose our jobs, or worse, if they felt our
activities were harmful to the state.

Still I continued to preach twice on Sunday and once
during the week, in addition to my job as a tailor in a
factory that made men's suits and coats. Then a
directive was handed down from the government: only
those who had a license from the government could
preach, and they would have to go to the police each
month and show this license in order to preach for the
next month. I was not given a license. I still don't know
why.

"What are you going to do, Sandor?" Ester asked me
nervously.

I went to the window and looked out over the
snow-packed street. More than sixty people worshiped
at our church, and they needed someone to lead
them: to encourage them in their faith and to explain
the Bible. I turned slowly to her.

"The church wants to ordain me. I have to give them
my answer tonight."

Fear leaped to her eyes, and for a time she was silent.
She did not ask me to refuse, but I could see how
disturbed she was. "What are you going to do?"

"I don't know." I came back to where she was standing
and placed my hands on her shoulders. "I've been
asking God what I should do."

I knew what I wanted to do, what I would do if it were

left to me. I had been in concentration camps so long, I panicked when I even thought of having to go back. Yet, those people needed me. If God wanted me to be their pastor, how could I refuse?

At the meeting that night, I gave them my decision. "I have the faith that God can take care of me," I said. "I will accept."

But once they learned I had not been given a license, their joy turned to concern. They decided they could not ask me to be ordained.

But the law said nothing about praying. So we got together as we always did and sang a few songs and read the Bible, with no one in particular leading us. Then we knelt to pray. When we were on our knees, I would give the message with the congregation kneeling around me.

In those days the church was growing rapidly. I have always suspected that was the thing that called our little group to the attention of the people who lived around the church, and particularly the party faithful. One man came often, asking questions and appearing to be genuinely interested and concerned about the ministry. No one really knew who he was or the purpose for this interest. We only suspected his true motives.

He discovered who our members were and attended our services and got acquainted with several. The most devastating informant was an elderly widow who didn't realize what she was doing. She was not a member, but was excited about the church and loved us all. She thought the man was merely another Christian. In Hungary, believers were a tightly knit, little cluster, and often visited other Christians when they were in their area, whether they were personally acquainted or not.

"The church is going very well," this elderly lady said when the man visited her. "Sandor Berger is preaching, and he's a wonderful man. Sometime when you are here on a Sunday, you should stop by and see how many worship with us and why everyone loves Brother Berger so."

From that time on I was watched closely.

The government reestablished the court system, and made much of the fact that people were not being imprisoned without proper charges and a guilty verdict.

An outspoken member of a church not far from ours was lured into speaking his mind in an open portion of their service. That night he was arrested and taken away from his family. There were those who also tried to get me to speak out against the government, but I had long since learned to remain silent.

I knew nothing of the information that elderly woman had so innocently given the party member. All I knew was that the attitude of the plant manager where I worked suddenly turned against me. He wanted me to put in less hours than before; but at the same time I was given a larger quota than the other workers—because I was faster, he explained awkwardly.

I didn't have to be told how important it was for me to meet that quota every day. I knew how serious my position would be if I fell behind. To cut my hours on the job was an insidious way of making me miss my quota.

Always before, the manager and I had gotten along very well. We had respect for each other. I knew him to be a just and good man; he knew me to be faithful at my job. Now, however, things were different. He started quarreling and fighting with me. "You have a bad feeling for me, Berger," he accused. "You're trying to start trouble."

I assured him I still had the same respect for him, and that I had said nothing to any of the workers to start trouble. However, he wouldn't listen.

"You are sloppy in your work, and you don't keep the floor clean around your bench. You are going to have to do better, or I will be forced to report you."

The next few weeks I tried even harder than before, but it didn't seem to do any good. The excuses to interfere with my work continued: "There is a problem with the material you should be using today," I would be told. Or, "We are changing patterns for you and the new ones didn't come in. You had just as well stay home." Or there was something wrong with my sewing machine that might cause it to drop stiches and turn out inferior work. I was not to use it until the repairman had checked it out.

Someone without my Nazis experience might not have been suspicious, but I knew what they intended. I had been given a quota of work to turn out; if I didn't accomplish it, they would accuse me of sabotage, of undermining the state's economic progress.

Next the plant manager changed my hours to Saturday night. I was to come to work when the rest of the clothing factory was closed and stay on the job through to Sunday morning. They gave me a key to a side door, and a bolt of material was put out for me. Although they always had some reason for doing what they did, I was aware that it was just an excuse. The plant manager was firm in his determination to make it impossible for me to produce as much work as before. But regardless of what he did, the Lord helped me to meet my quota. I didn't see how I could get so much accomplished in such a short time, but always when the time came for me to leave the plant, I had done all that I was supposed to.

But one Saturday night I went down to the plant and found the door locked against me. The bolt had been thrown, making it impossible for me to get in with my key. I had no other way of getting to my bench, and there was no one around to let me in. For a brief instant I panicked.

I went from one window to another, looking for one that was unlocked. *Dear God!* I prayed. *Help me!*

I had almost given up when I reached the men's rest room at the back of the building. There, a small window was unlatched. Thankfully I crawled through it.

I had lost so much time getting into the building I was sure I would be unable to make my quota. I was undone. Finished. When the manager had this evidence, I would be branded as an enemy of the state. As I worked, frantically, I prayed, asking God's help and strength and courage.

When Sunday morning came and it was time for me to go home, I had finished the required amount of work. Don't ask how I was able to do it. Without the help of the Lord, I would have failed.

Monday morning the manager called me into his office. "Why didn't you get your quota finished last week?" he demanded angrily.

I could feel his gaze burning into mine, the same way the guards in the Nazi camps glared at me when they were issuing orders. "I'm going to have to report this!"

"But I did make my quota," I protested.

His lower jaw sagged. "You couldn't have!"

"Come out and see."

Numbly he followed me out to my workbench and I showed him what I had done over the weekend. He was incredulous. "But—but how?"

If I hadn't known before, I would have known then that I had been purposely locked out. It was to have been the final link in a chain that would have bound me as an enemy of the people, the most serious crime of all, according to our new government.

A few days later the manager told me that he was going to be transferred to a large clothing factory in another area. "I'm sorry to have you leave," I said sincerely. "I have appreciated you as a friend and a supervisor. I'm going to miss you." And that was true. Before he had started harassing me, he had been a good person to work for.

A strange look darkened his eyes and he turned away. When I left the building that evening, he joined me. We walked together through the park.

"I thought you would be angry for the way I have treated you," he murmured, keeping his voice low so that someone even a few feet away would have been unable to hear.

"No," I answered, "I'm not angry with you. I wish you could take me with you."

He stopped on the narrow walk, eyeing me uneasily. Something had happened to him that I did not understand. Then he changed the subject abruptly.

Keeping his voice just above a whisper, he said, "I'm

going to tell you the whole truth, Berger. I'm going to tell you why you've been working on Saturdays instead of having the same hours as the rest of the men.

"You are preaching without a license, and they are anxious to put you in jail. But they need another reason, so they've been pressuring you on the job. They want to find you guilty of sabotage."

I was surprised to hear him speak so openly.

"You know how things are arranged, don't you?" he continued. "There are eleven people in each group or cell, and each person is directed to inform on the other ten."

I nodded silently.

"The people in our country are being watched constantly. Government eyes are in the factories, in the shops, and in the homes. On Sunday you should not stay at home. Let someone else preach in your church. Go out into the country to different churches if you have to speak, and never to the same one too often."

"They should check the work I am doing," I said. "They will find I am working as I am supposed to," I reminded him.

I had not been at the factory for more than a few hours the next Monday morning when I had visitors: two men who came to check my work. They stood by my bench as I sewed, saying little to me when they came and nothing when they left. I thought that was quite odd, especially when they returned again in two or three hours, as though to verify the fact that I was working at the same speed. I had done far more work than the regular quota for tailors in a similar period of time, but I can't take credit for that. God made it possible.

When they saw how much I was doing, they were amazed and gave me a medal, which signified that I had earned the highest award for production. Quite different from calling me to the court and putting me on trial.

After this I never preached in our own church, or attended there regularly. Yet, even in this, God had a plan. The little church in the country where I went to preach had no pastor and could not afford to pay a full-time man. Because one had to travel by train and on foot for several hours to get there, no one else would preach at this country church.

All during the week I would get up at five o'clock in the morning to pray and study for the next Sunday's services. On Sunday I got up at the same time and left home as early as possible in order to get to the church by 9:30, in time for Sunday school.

At first I had not been able to understand why God would allow another persecution to attack me, but after years of joyful service in that little church, I began to understand his wisdom. Had it not been for the Communists, I would have missed the joy of serving where God wanted me.

SIXTEEN   An Unresolved Question

TIBOR VAGO

After the war, I began to ask Ida to go out with me. I loved her, even before our first evening alone. It seemed as though I had always loved her and although we didn't talk about it, I had reason to believe that she cared for me. However, we didn't have a serious commitment to each other until I was attending the university. In 1950 we became officially engaged.

In Hungary, the engagement is different than in America. It is a family occasion, almost as important as the marriage ceremony. Wedding rings are exchanged and worn on the left hand. At the marriage ceremony they are moved to the right hand.

My parents joined with Ida's in giving a little engagement party for our relatives. The next Sunday it was announced in church.

We wanted to be married in our own church, but Mr. Berger asked us not to. It was wiser, he reasoned, to have a quiet wedding in one of the smaller country churches nearby. The party had left him alone by this time, and he saw no need in calling attention to the family again.

IDA

I had been accepted at the university, but changed my mind about going when I got married. After the wedding, we had to live with my parents. There was such a shortage of housing in Hungary that the law required a certain number of people to live in a house or an apartment with a certain number of rooms.

Through a pastor I had met at a youth conference, I learned of a prayer meeting that was being held in a different church. It had begun with young people, but was no longer just the college crowd. Christians of all ages and from all denominations came. There would be no problems, the pastor said. The meetings were held quietly in the church, and there were no big announcements. That, of course, was important to us. We had lived through so much, we were fearful of doing anything to cause trouble for us again.

It was at this prayer meeting that I met a charming woman about mother's age, a vivacious, well-read individual who handled English as well as she did German and Hungarian and walked very closely with her God. Although there was a great deal of difference in our ages, there was an affinity between us, a bond that was difficult to understand.

"Why don't I come out to your house one day?" she suggested.

"Why don't you?" I replied. And it was decided.

Mother had been ill and very discouraged, but she was feeling better when my friend came and was able to be up most of the time. We three women were sitting around the table when the subject of salvation came up. I am sure it was not an accident, but it all happened so casually we were not on guard.

"Are you saved?" my friend asked me pointedly. "If you were to die tonight, would you go to heaven?"

I felt my cheeks darken with embarrassment. All my life I had been tormented by that question. It had begun during World War II when I had seen death all around me. I was always afraid I would not go to heaven if I died, but I was unsure what to do about it—despite all papa had told me.

I was a good person, I reasoned. If I stole and lied and cheated or did other "bad" things, I would have something to confess, but I could see nothing in my life that I ought to tell God I was sorry for. I didn't realize that sin could be so-called little things.

Yet if everything was all right between myself and God, why did I have that empty feeling in my heart? Why would I waken at night and think about death fearfully?

In all the youth meetings I had attended, nobody ever said anything that helped me. At least I didn't hear it.

My father had preached salvation, and looking back, I don't see how I could have missed the meaning of his words. I seemed as though my ears were plugged against what he said.

Now this dear friend of mine asked me the question, her kindly gaze seizing mine and holding it. There was no way I could escape. "What would happen, Ida, if you were to die tonight?" she repeated. "Would you go to heaven?"

I was flustered and defensive at first, and if it had been anyone else I might have been angry in spite of the aching in my heart. But knew it was her love for me that caused her to speak.

I looked away, my fingers nervously encircling the coffee cup on the table in front of me. I lifted it from the bright cloth thoughtfully, but set it back without putting it to my lips. "I don't know for sure," I admitted. I tried to speak calmly, but my voice trembled. My eyes swept the room in one quick glance and focused on her lined face. "How can you *know*?" I asked seriously.

Now both my mother and my friend knew that all those years I had been playing a grim charade, pretending to be something I wasn't. I wondered what they would think of me. I soon learned that my friend was not surprised, nor did she think any less of me.

"How shall I know?" I asked her.

"Read John 3:16," she said, opening her Bible and laying it before me.

"No," she stopped me. "Read it this way: "For God *SO* loved the world he gave his only begotten Son that whosoever believeth on him should not perish but have everlasting life."

I had heard that verse more times than I could count and had memorized it before I started school, but I had never quite understood it the way I did that afternoon. Still, I wasn't quite sure that I could claim what it said as being for me. My friend must have known what I was thinking, for she did not stop there.

"Now read the eighteenth and thirty-sixth verses of the same chapter."

I read aloud, "He that believes on him is not condemned; but he that believes not is condemned already, because he has not believed in the name of the only begotten Son of God. He that believes on the Son has everlasting life; and he that believes not the Son, shall not see life; but the wrath of God abides on him."

She studied my taut face. "Do you believe in the Son?"

"I do."

"Then what does it say?" she persisted.

"It says if I believe, I have eternal life."

She leaned forward intently. "Do you, Ida? Do you have it?"

I read the verse once more. "According to this, I do."

But she was not finished yet. She took back the Bible and turned to 1 John 5:13: "These things have I written unto you that believe on the name of the Son of God; that you may know that you have eternal life."

She showed me other Bible verses to build up my faith, such as 1 John 1:9: "If we confess our sins, he is faithful and just to forgive us our sins."

I had been baptized at the age to twelve and had thought then that I was a Christian. It could be that I was right, and I only received assurance of my faith when my older friend talked with mama and me. Yet, I don't think I truly understood what it was to confess and receive Christ until that afternoon. There was a joy in my heart that I had never before experienced.

ESTER

Like Ida, I had gone to church all my life. I had listened to the minister every Sunday when I was growing up, and could quote as many Bible verses as anyone else. I had had many opportunities to hear the salvation story and receive Christ.

Those who knew me, including Sandor, thought I was saved. There were times when I thought so too. However, when I was more honest with myself, I had to admit a nagging fear of death. I looked at my husband, so serene and confident in his faith, and I was almost angry with him because I lacked his composure. If death came, he *knew* that he would be with Christ. There was no uncertainty in his heart, no wavering in his mind. Even during the darkest hours in the death camp, he was fully convinced that he would be with Jesus Christ when he died.

But I had nothing other than despair. The sermons I had heard had not touched me. Like Ida, my ears were plugged. I heard the words. I could find the texts in my Bible and do an acceptable job of deceiving everyone, except myself.

I reached menopause in 1955 and was sicker than most women during that time. I lay in bed, finding it difficult even to talk. But I thought. What was going to happen to me if I died? Finally I got enough courage to ask Sandor about my doubts and questions.

"Yes, yes," he answered quickly, thinking I only needed reassurance. "Of course you will go to heaven, Ester. You are a Christian."

That day Ida's friend visited us, I listened carefully as she explained how to receive Christ and be assured of eternal life with him. I was somewhat surprised to learn that Ida had the same problem I had, but I was so wrapped up in what our visitor was saying I really didn't think about it until later. As the women talked I finally understood what I had to do to be saved.

When she directed her attention to me, I was prepared for her question. When I, too, admitted my uncertainty, she went over the Bible verses again for me. But it wasn't necessary. I was now one of God's children. My heart was crying for joy that the matter was finally settled. I was a Christian as Sandor had believed me to be all the years we had been married!

SEVENTEEN The Revolution

SANDOR

The years before Stalin died in 1953 were difficult for everyone. Stalin had always been ruthless, but near the end of his rule he launched a purge that had eastern Europe awash in blood. It was almost as though he saw that the end of his own life was near, and he wanted to get as many of his real and fancied enemies as he could while he was still able to do so.

It was the same in our country. Soldiers and secret police were everywhere. Workers were forced to gather frequently to listen to lectures. At the close of each meeting, we were expected to clap our hands and chant,

"Long live Stalin. Long live Stalin."

At one meeting, the man next to me was clapping with the rest of us, but saying, "Die soon, Stalin. Die soon, Stalin," in a voice audible only to a few of us around him. I feared for him, because I knew the pitiless adversary we were facing when one of the men who was on the platform came down at the close of the meeting and sought him out. "What did you say just now?"

The fellow's face blanched. He had done it as a joke. Only at that moment did he realize the risk he had been taking. "The same as everybody else," he lied. "Long live Stalin."

The stranger moved closer. "No, you didn't. I read your lips." Then in a hoarse whisper he warned, "Be careful, my friend. Be very careful."

Stalin died quite soon after that, and with his passing there was a relaxation of controls. The soldiers and secret police were still very much in evidence, yet there was a change. In 1955 people could travel out of the country for the first time since World War II. Going to the West was not forbidden if one were visiting the Communist countries to the south or the east. And we were no longer in danger of being imprisoned. It began to look as though we might one day have a measure of the freedom we enjoyed before the Germans ruled over us.

IDA

Yet we were still apprehensive that another Hitler or a different Stalin might take over our country and throw

us into persecution once more. For papa and me
especially, that thought was never far from our minds.
Hungary's long history as a battlefield for Europe, and
our own experiences with the Nazis and Stalin still
clouded our thoughts.

The week before the revolution of 1956, God seemed
to tell me to read the book of Isaiah almost
continuously. Again and again I went to chapter 54.
That portion became a promise to me and my family.
Verses 13 and 14 were particularly meaningful: "All
your sons shall be taught by the Lord, and great shall be
the prosperity of your sons. In righteousness you shall
be established. You shall be far from oppression and you
shall not fear, and far from terror, for it shall not come
near."

I began to think about leaving Hungary to get to some
country in Europe that was out of the historical
battlefield, someplace where we could live and rear our
children without the threat of being engulfed in war.

There was another verse that caught my attention,
too. I can't remember where it was found or the exact
words, but in the Hungarian Bible it goes something
like this: "It is little to me that you are disciples here in
Judea, but I will send you away, that my message will go
through you all over the world."

Those verses seemed to be telling me that we would
get to the West so we could serve in the salvation of many
throughout the world. That hardly seemed possible.
Father was a tailor and part-time minister. Tibor was
well educated, but holding a secular job. Mama and I
were housewives. The idea that we would ever
accomplish anything for the Lord, except on a local

basis, seemed ridiculous. It even seemed crazy to think that we would be able to leave Hungary. We had little money to travel to the part of Europe where we would be safe from the dangers of war or persecution. Yet the feeling persisted.

At first I said nothing to anyone about my dreams. However, at the little cottage prayer meeting in our home where I felt especially close to the people, I shared what was on my mind. When I finished telling how the Lord had been dealing with me, there was a brief silence. Then the woman who had led mama and me to salvation reached over and laid a hand on my knee. "Ida," she said quietly, "when you go, take care of us."

There was no doubt in her voice that we would be going. She accepted it without question. I knew well what she meant. If we went to the West and prospered, we must help those who remained to spread the gospel of Jesus Christ.

Even though God had placed the assurance on my heart, the thought seemed so preposterous that I broke out laughing. And so did the others. I suppose I was as scornful as Sarah when she was told that she would bear a child in her old age. All week I had been tingling with a strange, exhilarating expectancy, waiting for each new day with anticipation and joy. Yet when someone else spoke as though she believed it, I saw how weak my faith was. I believed, and yet I disbelieved. I am so thankful that God's work to get us out of Hungary depended upon his marvelous loving-kindness and not my faith.

At the end of the meeting we began talking about the great concentration of students we had seen marching down the streets of the city. It was October 23, 1956, and none of us expected that this march would flare into bloodshed.

Several members of the prayer group had pamphlets they had been handed, detailing the demonstrators' demands. I don't know how the students managed to get their hands on a mimeograph machine and turn out the literature they distributed. Nor do I know how the movement spread beyond the academic community. It seemed to be spontaneous. People saw the demonstrators and joined them impulsively. Before the afternoon was over, men and women of all ages and all walks of life were caught up in it. A huge crowd poured into the park and tore down the huge statue of Stalin, breaking off pieces as souveneirs.

SANDOR

When we all got home that night, Tibor read the students' leaflet aloud to us, then commented, "The demands are not unreasonable. Maybe the government will grant them. That would open travel with the West, and we would be able to leave."

Ida was excited by the prospect. However, I did not agree.

"*Nem*," I said firmly. "It will not be that way. Look what the Nazis promised us. And the followers of Stalin. No one will be allowed to go."

Tibor challenged me. "Look what they have done since Stalin died. There have been many good changes. You have to admit that."

"*Igen*, I know." I wanted to believe he was right, but the spectre of Mauthausen was always before me, and the stories of Stalin's cruelty were indelibly etched in my mind.

We turned on the radio, eager for news. At ten o'clock the announcement came: the students' demands were completely unacceptable.

I looked over at Ida. The same fear that gripped me was reflected in her eyes. Once more I had visions of being separated from my family and being deported alone, without water or food. I was back in the death camp. I trembled inwardly.

In the next few days, the revolt swept the entire country like a gigantic tidal wave. Men, women, and children rose up against the government.

The history books tell what happened then. The powerful Soviet army seemed stunned by the fury of the attack. The people fought on, with twelve- and fourteen-year-old boys making Molotov cocktails and risking their lives to throw them at armored cars, tanks, and weapons carriers.

Ida was as disturbed by what was happening as I. We had been through so very much, we dreaded more uncertainty and bloodshed. It was not that either of us doubted God's ability to protect us. Far from it. We were concerned about our own mental and physical strength. As the battle worsened and surged around us, we went down into an air raid shelter in an effort to hide. Hungarian civilians were fighting in our very neighborhood—so close we could hear the flat, thin explosion of rifles and the rumble of tanks.

Remembering the way the Nazis used the radio when

they were in control, we listened to Radio Free Europe for the news. Two weeks after the fighting started, there was a startling announcement. The Russians had come to an agreement with the rebel leaders and the battle stopped. They were going to allow free elections, and most of the other student demands were to be granted.

Rejoicing, we came out of our shelter. But it was not to last long. Although the Russians had stopped fighting and there was peace within the city, they had not gone back to Rusia. They were merely waiting for reinforcements.

During this time God gave Ida another Bible verse. It is good that he gave it to her in Hungarian, I think. Our language has a slightly different meaning for the verse than the King James version, which says, "Depart ye, depart ye, go up from thence. . . . For ye shall not go out with haste, nor go by flight; for the Lord will go before you; and the God of Israel will be your reward." (Isa. 52:11, 12).

The Hungarian Bible says that you shall go, but you shall not run. Ida took this to mean that we were to leave Hungary, but it would be in a decent, orderly manner.

ESTER

During the days of the revolution, we talked often in the hush of our home about going to America and being reunited with my parents, who had moved there in 1945. But we always came back to the same problem. It would be impossible for us to get to the border. The trains weren't running, and we had no car.

We were discussing it one night when a friend came over to visit. We said nothing to him about our dream of leaving. However, before he left he expressed an interest in getting some of our furniture.

"If there is anything we can do to help you," he volunteered at the door, "Just let us know."

As soon as he was gone, Tibor called us together excitedly. "He's got a motorcycle.!"

"And he probably wants to keep it," Ida replied.

But you heard what he said about our furniture. Maybe we could make a trade with him."

At first it sounded as though God was providing us with a means of leaving the country.

"I could take two out on the motorcycle," Tibor suggested, "and come back for the others."

As we discussed that possibility, it soon became apparent that it was not as wise as it seemed. A motorcycle would be good for one or two, or maybe three, but there were five of us. And we had decided that whatever we did, we were not going to separate: part of us were not going to be in the West and the others in Hungary.

After the revolution quieted, we were able to go to church on Sunday morning or afternoon, but were not permitted to hold a meeting at night because of the curfew. For that reason, Ida and Tibor invited a friend and his wife over for the early evening. It was not until the guests had their coats on, however, that they mentioned that some people we knew were planning to leave the next morning.

"They're going to gather at a food company where one of the trucks will take them to the border," he said. "The truck has to make the trip to pick up Red Cross food and medical supplies and bring them back to Budapest."

"Do you think they would have room for us?" Tibor asked quickly.

'If you want to go," he replied, "just show up at the warehouse at six in the morning."

When their friends were gone, Tibor called Sandor and I into the living room and told us what had happened. He was so excited, he had difficulty in speaking. "We've asked God for an answer," he cried. "Now we have it. A way to travel to the border!"

I got my Bible. "We've all been praying for God's guidance. I want to read you the verse he gave me this afternoon. 'Why do you cry to me? Step on the water.'"

But Sandor did not want to leave. "Your mama and I are getting old," he said. "We have little time left before God calls us home. Tibor, take Ida and your little girl in the morning and go to Austria and America if you can. You are young. You will have time to make new lives for yourselves." He paused for a moment, looking sadly at them. "We will stay here."

"No!" Ida broke in harshly. "We are a family. We are going to stay together. If we go to Austria and America, we all go. We are not going to separate from each other again on this earth."

Tibor and I agreed with her. The decision to leave would have to be unanimous, or we would not go.

EIGHTEEN   Across the Border

SANDOR

We sat in the living room of our little home, asking each other the same question over and over again: Would it be better to stay or should we try to leave the country?

By nature I am apprehensive and cautious, particularly after my experiences with the Nazis. Besides, mama and I were getting old, our daughter was pregnant, and we had a three-and-a-half-year-old granddaughter to think about. How would I feel if we tried to leave and got into trouble? There was no easy answer for us.

Ida picked up the Bible and thumbed its pages thoughtfully. In Jeremiah she found a verse that spoke to her heart. It was one of those verses she knew, but was unsure of the exact wording or where it was found.

But that didn't matter to us. We had prayed, "Lord, give us a Scripture we can stand on." A few minutes later it came to her. The people of Israel had been taken captive, she said, but God was speaking personally to Jeremiah. "You do what you want. If you want to go to Babylon, you can go. If you want to stay in your own country, you can stay. Whatever you think is best, you should do and I will be with you."

In a way, the verse was no help. It didn't dictate what we should do. What we had wanted was a sign that God would guide us in a course of action. Instead, he was telling us to do whatever we felt was best.

"If we do go," I said uneasily, "we will only get as far as the Austrian border. The Hungarian side is heavily mined. We'll risk getting a leg blown off, or worse."

"Not any more," Tibor broke in. "We heard over the radio that the mines have been taken up."

"There are too many things that can go wrong," I protested. "God saved me during the war and the persecution. He can take care of us right where we are." But none of the others seemed to agree so I added, "But if you all decide you want to go, I will go too." I shrugged indifferently, as though I didn't care what they decided. But that was not true. I was deeply concerned about the risk. We went to bed that night unsure of what we should do.

IDA

Lying in bed I had a talk with the Lord, silently, so even Tibor did not hear. *We have to be at the warehouse at six o'clock tomorrow morning, I said. If my daughter wakes up early enough to get there in time, we will take it as a sign that you want us to go. If she sleeps, we will remain here.*

Normally she was a late sleeper, so I was probably trying to give the Lord a little nudge in the direction I wanted to go.

We got our answer at five o'clock the next morning when our little girl woke up with diarrhea.

That wasn't exactly what I had been praying for, but there was no denying that she was awake, whimpering fretfully.

From that moment on, I had no doubts about God's leading. We were to leave Budapest on this day, November 19, 1956.

My parents had been talking, however, and they were sure we ought to stay in Hungary. While we were discussing the matter, mama turned on the radio, and we listened to the newscast.

"Russian soldiers have crossed the Hungarian border and are moving on Budapest."

Tibor got to his feet and paced across the well-worn kitchen floor. "If we wait even twenty-four hours, it may be too late."

That helped us decide. We scrambled to get our things ready. I didn't have a pair of slacks, so I put on a pair of my father's pants and two dresses of mine. It was cold in Hungary at that time of year, and we knew there would be no heat in the back of the truck. I got some clothes for the baby while my parents finished packing.

We had one bicycle for the four of us. While the rest of us walked on ahead, Tibor stayed behind to get some important papers and some honey and bread. Then he locked the house and rode the bicycle to the place where a truck was to pick us up and take us to catch another truck for the border. He came peddling up just as our transportation arrived.

Once we arrived at the warehouse, the food-company driver took his time preparing to leave. We got there at six in the morning as we were supposed to, and the driver did not pull out until one o'clock in the afternoon. As the hours dragged on, the nervous tension engulfed us.

Finally the truck left the warehouse, but instead of heading directly out of the city, the driver drove back up our street to get something in the neighborhood. We moved slowly past the store on the corner where we did much of our shopping. If we had craned our necks, we would have seen our house; but none of us even looked. We hunched there miserably, fighting the temptation to shout for the driver to stop so we could go back home.

A thousand unanswered questions still drove like spikes in our minds. However, we remained silent, and in a few moments we were rumbling away from the area toward the city limits.

There were twenty of us sitting on the back of the open truck. We would have been self-conscious and afraid under a canvas covering. Exposed as we were, we were terrified. All the bridges had been carefully guarded since the time of the Nazi occupation. Any soldier or police officer could get suspicious and stop us for questioning. When he asked, "Where are your papers?" we would be caught, for none of us had the proper papers to leave Budapest.

But the driver was more experienced than we had realized. He would go around the city until he reached a small, out-of-the-way crossing that was sparsely guarded. The two guards who were there didn't stop us. Why? Only our Lord knows the answer. This was the first of many miraculous slights in procedure that characterized that day.

Once across the river our driver found some rope, and we stopped briefly to fasten the canvas securely in place. Once it was above us, the canvas provided some protection against the wind and shielded us from view. But we were not out of danger. If the truck were stopped, as it surely would be, it would be searched.

The driver left the highway shortly after crossing the river and sought out narrow country roads that would be less dangerous. He kept us informed of the upcoming village so we would not appear ignorant if the guards questioned us.

TIBOR

We were stopped the first time shortly after we crossed the river. The soldiers talked briefly with the driver, then they came to the rear of the truck and lifted a corner of the canvas cautiously and looked in.

"Identification?"

We got out our papers to prove that we were Hungarians. But the soldiers scarcely looked at them. The guards manner conveyed something I had never expected. Fear! Imagine being afraid of a truck filled with unarmed men, women, and children! God had put that fright in their hearts. I was still concerned about our safety, but I was also rejoicing. Our Lord was with us! He was answering our prayers each step of the way.

Later when we were stopped at another checkpoint. One of the Russian soldiers pulled back the canvas and asked, "*Zima Zima?* Are you cold?"

We nodded wordlessly, hesitant to say anything unless we had to.

"*Dosvidani.*" He motioned the truck to go on with a wave of his rifle. "See you again," he said as we pulled off without having to show anything but the driver's papers, which were in order.

The next time we were stopped by Hungarian rather than Russian soldiers. Brusquely they ordered us out of the truck. We all obeyed, except Ida who remained seated with our little daughter on her lap.

"You," the offcer exclaimed, motioning her to the rear. "Get out too!"

"But she's pregnant!" I protested. "Don't you see?" The officer acted as though he hadn't even heard me. "Out of the truck."

"Look at her!" I said loudly. "She's pregnant. We have a little girl and we don't have any food. We have to get to the country!" Tears came to my eyes as I pleaded with him.

"Where are the papers for you to leave Budapest?"

"We don't have any."

"Then you go no farther!" He was impersonal, as though he was telling us we could not travel on a certain street. "The truck can go on. The driver has the proper papers. The rest of you have to go back!"

I looked at Ida and our little girl. How could they walk

back to Budapest in such cold weather? They would die! And what of Papa and Mama Berger and the others?

Tears ran down my cheeks as I begged him to let us go on. "What is there for us to go back for? We will die."

For an instant he hesitated and I was sure that we were finished. Then his face softened, and he, too, motioned us back into the truck. "All right," he said, gruffly. "Go!"

We scrambled back into the vehicle and continued on our way, praising God. The soldiers had to have known where we were going. I still don't see how they allowed us to go on, except that God worked a miracle in their hearts when they saw my wife's condition.

Earlier that year she had miscarried a baby. If that little one had lived, he would have been a few months old at the time of the revolution. We would not have been able to flee with two small children. How many times we have marveled at how God timed and used this event!

We were stopped repeatedly by other Hungarian guards, and each encounter was an agonizing experience. They had complete authority over us. Instead of turning us back, they chose to allow us to go on. Again and again we saw the marvelous, loving hand of God.

Finally the truck driver stopped in a town a few kilometers from the border where there were people waiting for him. "This is as far as I go," he said. "From here you are on your own."

As we got out, a merchant and his family approached us with an air of authority. "Don't go over the border tonight, he said. "We heard some shooting earlier."

But a young unmarried couple who came with us

were unwilling to wait. "I've got a sister in the West," the boy said, as though he had to have some reason for haste. "We're going to cross tonight."

Our self-appointed host made no attempt to stop them. We never learned if they made it, because we didn't see them again. But the rest of us went home with our new friend and waited.

Once we were all seated comfortably in his living room, he explained the plan and invited us to spend the night with him. "I'm the only one in town who has a phone," he said. "My friend in the next village, closer to the Austrian border, has one too. Tomorrow morning I will call and find out when it will be safe for you to go."

I didn't even think of the possiblility of his betraying us. We were so positive that God had his hands in ours that we trusted our new friend as one sent to watch over us.

Later we were taken to one of the two bedrooms, a small cubicle no more than four meters square. Almost before we sat down, there were others coming to seek the merchant's help. They came by couples and families as truck after truck pulled into the village and discharged their human cargo.

I don't know where they all spent the night. At least forty crowded into the little room where we were, standing so close to each other we could scarcely breathe. No one slept. We were talking endlessly.

Finally daylight came, and noon, and at last nightfall. We didn't know who we were waiting for or what signal would be given, but everything was well organized. When the time came for us to leave, Ida and our daughter and I were taken to the nearby railroad tracks first, to head the line. After standing there a while waiting, I looked back, astonished to see the tracks behind me jammed with hundreds and hundreds of people.

"If you hear a noise," our host warned, "there is to be no hysterics, no crying, no yelling. Lay down flat on your stomach and wait! Don't get upset or panic!"

The word as passed along tensely, from one to another throughout the long line. Then the man glanced at Ida and me. "Ready!" he asked softly.

We both nodded. I took our daughter on my shoulders and grasped Ida by the arm. We started forward slowly, picking our way over the frozen ground toward Austria and freedom. I had put a kerchief over our little girl's mouth before we started and warned her to be quiet. "Whatever you do," I told her, "don't make a sound. Understand?"

We had walked for a few minutes when our guide motioned us to stop until we heard from one who was walking even farther ahead. When he sent back word that the way was clear, we started forward once more.

We had been on the way for half an hour when our daughter leaned forward and put her tiny hands on my face to turn it so she could look at me. "You really are my papa, aren't you?" she whispered. Positioned on my shoulders, she was unable to see my face clearly. She was so afraid, she needed to make sure it was really me carrying her.

"*Igen*," I said, my voice choking with emotion. "I am your papa."

Reassured, She let go of my face and we continued to move forward in the darkness.

I looked back at Papa Berger now and then. His lean face was taut, and I saw that his lips were moving silently. It was comforting to know that both he and Mama Berger were praying as I was. Somehow I had more confidence in their prayers than my own. That might not be scriptural, but they seemed so close to God that I felt he might answer their petitions before mine.

Finally our guide stopped us and pointed to a ditch that lay directly in front of us. "See that?" he said tensely. "Cross it and you will be in Austria."

We took the Hungarian money we had in our pockets, our watches, and anything else of value and gratefully gave them to him. We wouldn't have had to. He asked for nothing. But we wanted to show our thankfulness.

Some of the people started to run forward, as though only a few might be accepted and they had to get there before the border closed. I might have run myself, but Ida was having trouble walking by this time. I had to help her across the ditch. I looked back at Papa Berger once more. Tears were streaming down his cheeks.

"We have made it!" he whispered, his words choking in his throat. "Thanks be to God!"

NINETEEN Perfect Peace

SANDOR

Once we were across the border, the Austrians, with the aid of American money, were well organized to feed and house us until we had the proper papers and a train ticket to Vienna. After about three weeks of traveling from the Austrian police to the American Embassy and the Church World Service to obtain our papers, we boarded a train for Vienna.

It was a long, hard, exhausting trip, but we were so caught up in the excitement of the past few days and were so confused and bewildered about the uncertainty of the future, we didn't notice how tired we were. That would come later, after we knew where we would be going and how we would manage to live.

We had never been wealthy, but now we had nothing except the clothes we were wearing. Our home, our furniture, everything we owned was across the border in Hungary. We could never go back to get them.

Ester was deeply troubled about Ida. Our only daughter had one child to care for and was heavy with a second. The ordeal was more difficult for her than the rest of us. Her eyes were sunken and dark-rimmed with exhaustion, and a great weariness was evident in every move she made.

My wife did what she could to help with the little girl so Ida could get some rest. On one occasion, when she was caring for our granddaughter, Ida leaned back and closed her eyes momentarily. In an instant she was asleep.

In Vienna we were taken to a camp that had been hastily prepared for refugees like ourselves. There we were questioned in detail by representatives from the American embassy. They were kindly but insistent, talking to us privately and as a family. Our stories were checked, one against the other, until the officials were satisfied that we were telling the truth. It was a time of standing in line for what seemed to be hours, and then going from room to room where we repeated our stories over and over again.

We had difficulty understanding why there should be such skepticism and disbelief. After all, we were giving up everything to escape from Hungary. Why would they fear we were lying? One look at us ought to tell them everything they needed to know. At times we worried that this might be some sort of plot to keep us out of the country we had chosen. We didn't see how that could be, but the thought kept sneaking back to plague us.

Then other refugees told us the reason for the questioning: the Americans were afraid spies would be slipped into the country along with the rest of us. Now we could understand their concern. That didn't change the lengthy interrogations and delays, but it did make it easier for us to accept them. Finally, when the Americans were satisfied that we were legitimate refugees, we were given our immunization shots and told we could go to America. The United States had not closed its borders to the massive onslaught of refugees coming out of Hungary as Switzerland had. At last we were going to the West as we had dreamed.

We cried unashamedly.

But we had no money and nothing to sell so, like all the others, we would have been trapped in Austria had it not been for the generosity of the United States government. Air force planes flew us over the Atlantic to Fort Dix, New Jersey, without charge.

From there we were transferred to Camp Kilmore where the questioning was repeated. By this time we accepted it patiently. Then papers were filled out, and we were given green cards to indicate we could remain in America. But there was still one more requirement before we could leave the camp: we had to have sponsors willing to sign papers saying they would be responsible for us for a year.

Quickly we contacted Ester's mama and papa in New York; they not only sponsored us but also opened their home to us once we were released. From there Tibor and

I began to look for work.

I was still a good tailor and quickly got a job in one of New York's many garment factories. It happened so easily I could scarcely believe it. I knew only a little English at first, but was still able to get by. It was the same with my son-in-law. He got a job in a factory where they had a Hungarian-speaking foreman. It was not a very good job, but as he learned English he was able to find something that paid better and was more suited to his training and abilities.

Soon, I was preaching part-time again, and we would have been content to stay in New York for the rest of our lives, happy in our Lord and the complete freedom of America. But God had more for us.

Ida had told us how God had shown her that he had a great ministry for us. Ester and I had said little to her about it at the time, but we had not believed that possible. A little church such as we had in Hungary was the sort of work he wanted us to do, according to our thinking. We were content to have the opportunity to reach a soul for Christ occasionally or to be an encouragement to someone with a problem.

In 1960, a young Christian who was concerned about the Hungarian people went to a missionary radio station with enough power to reach far behind the Iron Curtain. He invited us to prepare messages in Hungarian to be beamed back to our beloved land.

But that was only the beginning. Ida and Tibor, with their deep interest in books, saw another opportunity for service. They began to translate and publish books in the Hungarian language. Thousands of copies have been sent into Hungary.

It has been more than twenty years since we left the land of our birth. The weeks and months in the work camps and finally the death camp are but an ugly dream. So is the loneliness and concern that gripped us all as we feared that another wave of Jewish persecution might engulf our children or our children's children.

We see now that God had a reason, a plan for our lives during all the suffering of World War II and the Stalin era. He has led us far from the home of our birth. Through everything that happened, God was with us. He set the limits beyond which Satan could not go. And I am firmly convinced that until our work here on earth is finished, we are immortal. He will keep us in perfect peace.

I used to wonder why God had brought us out of Hungary that fateful day in 1956. I hadn't really wanted to come, because I had the assurance of his Word that he would keep us safe whether we stayed or left. Now I know the answer to that nagging question, Why?—that question we asked ourselves so many times as we agonized over whether or not we should leave Hungary.

The words of Isaiah that God gave to Ida have literally come true. "I will give you for a light . . . that my salvation may extend to the end of the earth."

Messages in Hungarian have reached countless thousands who speak that language. Thousands of books have been mailed throughout the world. Testimonies, both spoken and written, have been an encouragement and a challenge to those who have spiritual needs. And there are constantly new opportunities—new horizons for us to run toward.

It is difficult for me to believe that God has chosen to

use us in the way he has. But he had a plan, and he patiently, tenderly guided us until we were usable. It is our prayer that our story may touch your life—that the reading of the way God provided for us will be an encouragement for you to place your complete trust in him.